WHY'S EVERYTHING SO DIFFICULT?
A YOUTH'S PERSPECTIVE TOWARDS LIFE

J K ARYA

BLUEROSE PUBLISHERS
India | U.K.

Copyright © J K Arya 2025

All rights reserved by author. No part of this publication may be reproduced, stored in a retrieval system or transmitted in any form or by any means, electronic, mechanical, photocopying, recording or otherwise, without the prior permission of the author. Although every precaution has been taken to verify the accuracy of the information contained herein, the publisher assumes no responsibility for any errors or omissions. No liability is assumed for damages that may result from the use of information contained within.

BlueRose Publishers takes no responsibility for any damages, losses, or liabilities that may arise from the use or misuse of the information, products, or services provided in this publication.

For permissions requests or inquiries regarding this publication, please contact:

BLUEROSE PUBLISHERS
www.BlueRoseONE.com
info@bluerosepublishers.com
+91 8882 898 898
+4407342408967

ISBN: 978-93-6783-874-7

Cover Design: Aman Sharma
Typesetting: Pooja Sharma

First Edition: February 2025

Author's note

Hey there, amazing soul! I know you're facing many challenges and working hard to make everything more efficient and purposeful. This book is your trusted companion on this journey, offering valuable insights along the way. Here, you'll discover various factors, difficulties, and problems that most champions like you face in their daily lives. I promise to be with you every step of the way, and I hope you'll find meaningful lessons to learn and implement as you engage with the powerful message this book aims to convey.

Dear Readers,

Thank you for being a part of my journey through this book. I hope it brings a positive change to your understanding and mindset about how we observe and live our lives. If this book resonates with you, I would love to hear your feedback or thoughts on anything important to you.

Feel free to connect with me as your Jitu Bhaiya, your friend.

Here's how you can reach me:

Instagram:- @Jitu_Arya21

Email:- jkarya054@gmail.com

Your love and support mean everything to me, and I look forward to hearing from you!

Warm regards,

J.K. Arya

Recognize the challenges life presents, acknowledge your strengths in overcoming them, appreciate your worth in taking risks, and embrace the reality that everything happens for a reason.

-J.K. ARYA

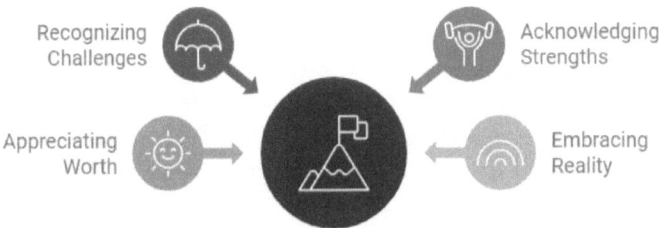

Introduction

Hello there, Wonderful champ, if you've got this book in your hands, you're probably curious about what makes it special. What exactly do you get to learn from it and how will it help you in making your life and your personality better?

This book isn't your typical read about big-shot entrepreneurs or famous folks. Nope, it's all about YOU—the youngster navigating the twists and turns of life. It's a dive into the minds of youngsters, exploring how they face everyday challenges that can disturb or even sometimes disrupt their lives making them feel "Why's everything so difficult". These challenges could be anything—your sense of humor, your thoughts, the stigma around certain habits, overthinking, and more.

Ever noticed how life messes with your humor, thoughts, or even your quirky habits? We're diving into the real stuff—overthinking, struggles, and some messy adventures of growing up from a carefree kid to a young adult juggling careers and love.

This isn't something like guidance from the high and mighty; it's like a chat with a friend who struggles. From teenage escapades to the wild world of bachelor life, we're exploring it all. Buckle up for a roadmap through the ups and downs, failures, achievements, and the beautiful chaos of it all.

I really want you to remember this message that it may not seem like a big deal to some, but it truly means a lot to me. That's why I poured my heart into writing this book. It delves into your emotions and explores how we navigate them as teenagers and young adults.

Engage with this text thoughtfully. Don't dismiss it as just another fleeting piece of content—like a quick YouTube short, Instagram reel, or a motivational post. Those things are created in moments, but this book represents my heartfelt effort to truly understand and connect with our generation. I've lived, observed, and poured my heart into this work, using real-life scenarios to bridge the gap between our experiences and understanding.

And I think this isn't just about understanding; it's about action. We're flipping the script on habits—tossing out the bad ones and picking up fresh awesome stuff. Expect some generous facts along the way—stuff you might know, stuff that'll make you go "Whoa!"

Navigating Youth Challenges for Personal Growth

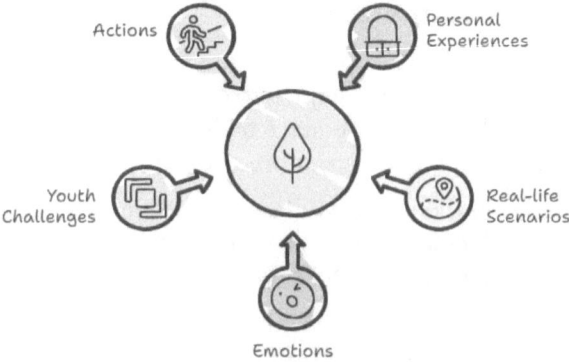

The Roadmap

I have organized the content into 24 different categories, with each category corresponding to a chapter that reflects the life cycle of today's generation. How a struggling champ feels when they fall down, become demotivated by not getting the expected outcome, or unfortunately get into any kind of traumatic situation. This book will ultimately help you to indulge yourself in the right way of dealing with and overcoming different situations by bouncing back.

It's about the wonders and the difficulties we get to enjoy in our lives.

Now you might be thinking how can anyone enjoy the difficulties of their lives?

The answer here should be on a positive note. Yes, my friend we can start enjoying our difficulties but it can happen only when we start taking it as a challenge that helps us to improve our future with our personalities.

Here in this book, we will learn the values that life concurs for us and look at what else we can implement from here to make it more meaningful to bring a sense of joy.

If we want to achieve something bigger, then first we have to leave our rigid attitude of bringing no change. We've to understand that with a rigid attitude, we can never move forward into any new explorative part of our lives.

And guess what? At the end of each chapter, you'll have a "To-Do List." Yes, we're turning these lessons into practical steps to make your life better, filled with positivity and perseverance.

This will upgrade your mindset and your understanding following a progressive journey if you read this book with a growth mindset.

Some legends say, "The world is wholly dependent upon a single hope" but never understand what that hope really means. Yes, this is life my friend, this is your life. If you are alive, if you are capable then there is hope. So here we're going to understand the rollercoaster of life where we cannot find a smooth path to move upon every time. But here's the key—<u>It's YOUR Rollercoaster</u>. From teenage escapades to adulting challenges, this self-help journey is your guide to making it awesome. So, let's embark on this adventure together. Get ready to uncover some truths, boost your understanding, and make this ride called life a thrilling one!

Cheers to the journey ahead!

HAPPY READING:)

Chapter outline

Chapter 1: Life - Do you know me?
- An Introduction to Life.

Chapter 2: Growing from Missteps
-The Contribution of Mistakes.

Chapter 3: Self Confidence
-The best outfit to Own for your inner self.

Chapter 4: Do we bounce back after Failures?
-A bounce back that empowers self-confidence.

Chapter 5: Fear of trying something new
-This is a new year if you gain value for something new.

Chapter 6: Our Purposeful Goals
-Live your dream by your choices and take action.

Chapter 7: Embracing Imperfections
-You're imperfect, but not alone.

Chapter 8: A Game of the Senses
-The cultivation of goodness from hardships.

Chapter 9: A Change for Goodness
-Igniting the Flame of Transformation.

Chapter 10: The Outcome of Patience
-With determination and patience, nothing is impossible.

Chapter 11 Emotional Intelligence
-Learn the ability to apply the acumen of emotions.

Chapter 12: The Power of Empathy

-An Ability to Sense Someone's Emotions.

Chapter 13: Don't just exist, live!

-Find your way to Get Out, Explore and Thrive.

Chapter 14: Mental Health

-Delve into the complexities of our thoughts and emotions.

Chapter 15: Suicidal Thoughts

-A hope in a situation that will help you rise again.

Chapter 16: The Social Media Life

-Not everything you perceive is real.

Chapter 17: Dreams & Determination

-Never settle for average.

Chapter 18: Satisfaction & its Enormous Feelings

-An enormous feeling to make the dream your reality.

Chapter 19: Meditation and Mindset

-What you need to know.

Chapter 20: Addictions and Their Impacts

-An Approach that drains Life.

Chapter 21: Follow the phenomena we learn

-Give your knowledge an application to life.

Chapter 22: Quality Determine Results

-A qualitative approach makes your results approachable.

Chapter 23: The Change and Its Consequences

-The change in you, determines the consequences.

Chapter 24: Spiritualism
-A belief in something beyond the self.
The 4d Framework: "Do," "Don't," "Doing," and "Done."
Acknowledgment

Contents

Chapter - 1: Life - Do you know me?......................... 2

Chapter - 2: Growing from missteps 8

Chapter - 3: Self-confidence 14

Chapter - 4: Do we bounce back after failures?............ 21

Chapter - 5: Fear of trying something new................. 29

Chapter - 6: Our purposeful goals 37

Chapter - 7: Embracing imperfection 45

Chapter - 8: A Game of the Senses 53

Chapter - 9: A Change for Goodness 62

Chapter - 10: The outcome of patience................... 68

Chapter - 11: Emotional intelligence 74

Chapter - 12: The power of empathy 81

Chapter - 13: Don't just exist, live!....................... 89

Chapter - 14: Mental health 97

Chapter - 15: Suicidal thoughts........................... 106

Chapter - 16: The social media life 117

Chapter - 17: Dreams & determination................... 127

Chapter - 18: Satisfaction & its enormous feeling 132

Chapter - 19: Meditation and mindset................... 139

Chapter - 20: Addictions and their impacts............... 147

Chapter - 21: Follow the phenomena we learn............. 154

Chapter - 22: Quality determine results............................ 161

Chapter - 23: The change and its consequences 164

Chapter - 24: Spiritualism 168

The 4D framework 175

Acknowledgment 178

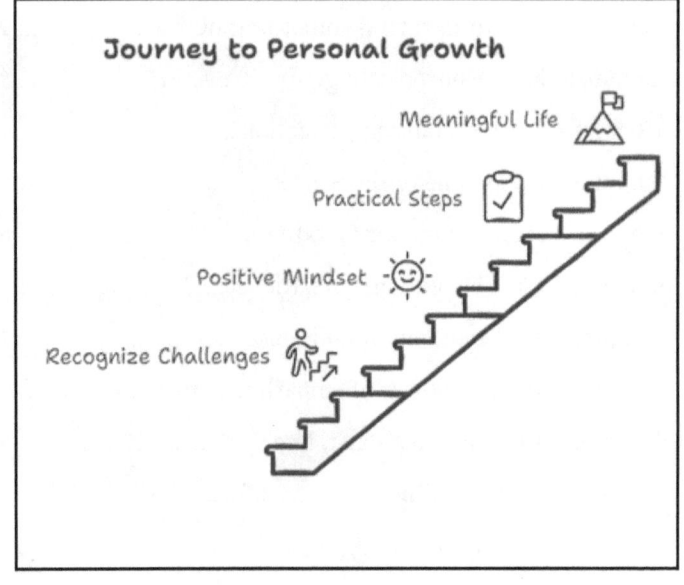

The three fundamentals of life: -

*Don't Forget Who Is Helping You
*Don't Hate Who Is Loving You
*Don't Cheat Who Is Believing You

—*Swami Vivekananda*

Chapter - 1
Life - Do you know me?

POV: "Before diving into the lessons, take a moment to let life make its introduction, like meeting someone new before starting a conversation. Be patient and allow this chapter to unfold, because sometimes, instead of facts and learning, what we actually need is a comfortable conversation to begin with. So, Life is offering a simple, meaningful message just for everyday people like you and me, waiting for your attention. Embrace it."

Hey champion, do you know who I am and how valuable I am to you?

Yes, I am the life you are living now, and I must say you are a champion in my field because you are trying to give your best in everything you are doing. You'll realize that there are so many things to learn and experience when you start understanding how important I am to you. You have already accomplished so many things that many others are still dreaming of.

Do you know why I called you a champion? It's because trying something new is not a small thing. I know very well that you are putting your best efforts into everything you want to achieve, but not every time you get the same results that you're striving for. It can feel awful, and sometimes it may disrupt your mind and cause your motivation down. But that's not the end, my friend. You need to understand that every day can't be the same and there'll arrive a day when you will realize that everything is making sense.

Do you know, champ, how you should focus on what life is offering you? You should focus on possibilities. Yes, you should focus on what you can control and what you can make happen in your life. All you need to see is what you have and what you can do. If you constantly focus on things that are out of your control, you may lose everything that is even within your control, the things that are yours, whether it's about any person, relationship, or career.

Therefore, do not burden yourself with events or actions that you have no control over. However, the time should be devoted more towards what you would like to gain in return. Oh, there are so many ways in which we can be knocked down emotionally—stress, anxiety and the tendency to overthink are just a few of them.

"Such emotions have the potential to halt your progress and success." Stress without seeking solutions hinders one from finding effective ideas and hence lowers productivity.

Now is the best time to think of how you will eliminate the barriers that slow you down. This will assist you in reaching your full potential to enable you to attain the sort of life you have always wanted.

That's why you shouldn't fear taking risks. Concentrate on the intention of why you wish to accomplish your goals and once you find that intention, give it a direction and just see how far it can take you.

I hope you don't forget that this moment is yours and nobody can deprive you of the opportunity to use everything that the world brings to you. It's always good to utilize different resources properly as every day (either good or bad) always has something to teach you if you choose to see the good things in it.

Here in our journey we've to understand that failure in planning leads to learning what is wrong and therefore the value of time is well understood. It becomes possible to make success a strong stimulus to get even higher results.

It means being self-centeredness and ignoring other people's opinions if it's not beneficial for you. This is your life, nobody else knows what is best for you more than you do. Remember, self-love requires strength. Do not be faithful in adherence to other's perceptions about life. Create it for yourself and be your own self because nobody understands you better than you do.

Many times, you will face challenges because that's what life is about. Without challenges, there is no growth, and there will be no difference between you and a non-living being. I think Facing challenges and meeting its solutions will make you grow and upgrade your vision to a higher level. I can assure you that when you succeed in solving problems or accomplishing your goals, you will be rewarded with appreciation and gifts that make you feel you've truly achieved something you dreamed of. That feeling, that happiness, will be an unbeatable emotion for you.

A REMINDER OF HOW TO APPROACH!

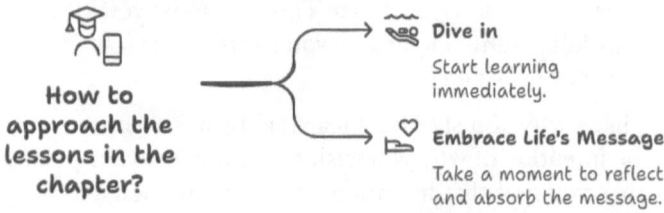

Let me share an incident with you.

Once, I attended a seminar with monks, businesspeople and students. During the event, a monk with a great knowledge and understanding about life's aspects asked the audience, "What is the meaning of life? "A wise man responded very quickly, and his response received applause from all around him. The response was, "Life has no meaning, it itself is an opportunity for us to create one." Everyone was mesmerized by his answer and started staring turning their head at him surprisingly.

Do you understand why the person responded that way? It's because life presents us with endless opportunities, testing our minds and rewarding us based on how we face challenges and tackle different problems. When we try to feed our brains with positivity and fill our hearts with love. When joy fills our lives, our minds will soar, guiding us toward the path and position we desire. This is true success—the real achievement in life.

People always ask, "What is the meaning of life?" "when they should be asking, "How can I make my life more meaningful?"

Let me explain with a simple example. On a sunny afternoon, a man rides his bicycle down a busy road. He spots someone on a scooter ahead and thinks, "If I only own that scooter, my ride would be easier." The scooter rider was a middle-aged man with his two children in the back seat and the sidecar, cruising smoothly, watching a hatchback car pass by, and dreaming of owning one for more comfort.

In the hatchback, the driver sees a flashy sports car and wishes they could drive something fast and stylish. But the sports car owner looks up at a private jet flying overhead and imagines the freedom of soaring above it all.

Each person, from the cyclist to the jet owner, wants what someone else has.

What we learn from these people is that no matter what we have, we rarely feel satisfied materialistically. We always wish for more, focusing on what others have that we don't. The lesson here is that we can never be satisfied with material things until we become content with our thoughts.

Life isn't something you figure out completely—it's always going to be a challenge. So, treat it with care, like raising a child. Take each step thoughtfully. Life might not always be fun, but don't let it be ordinary—make your journey unique and meaningful.

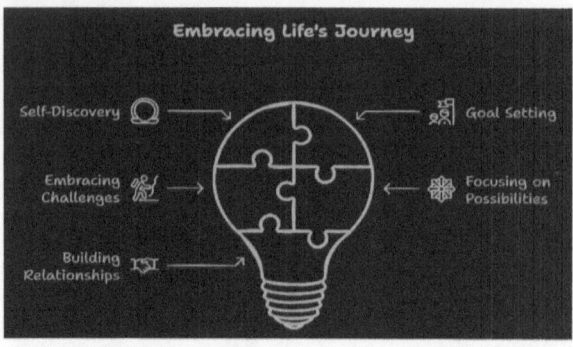

<u>*Shakespeare once said,*</u>

"I cried when I had no shoes, but I stopped crying when I saw a man without legs. Life is full of blessings, but sometimes we never evaluate them."

So, here we'll end the conversation with the hope that life has given you its best talk to make you understand what value you keep here and how we should make our minds thoughtful. Create each day better than the previous one. The past is beyond your control, but the future holds the potential to change everything.

And remember, miracles happen in everyone's life—once you start believing, you'll begin to see them.

<u>Here is a to-do list for you after this introductory chapter titled: "Life - Do You Know Me?":</u>

1. <u>Reflect on your values</u>: What is important to you?
2. <u>Identify areas of improvement</u>: This could be related to your health, relationships, career, or personal growth.
3. <u>Set goals</u>: Set realistic and achievable goals for yourself based on your values and areas of improvement.
4. <u>Practice self-care</u>: Take care of yourself physically, mentally, and emotionally.

5. <u>Build positive relationships</u>: Build positive and supportive relationships with people that impact your life and the environment around you.

By following this to-do list, you can apply the lessons taken from this chapter "Life - Do you know me?" to live a more fulfilling and meaningful life based on your values and priorities.

<u>LESSON</u>: - Every single day makes you realize that waking up with a sunrise is enough to see opportunities and you've to identify and make them meaningful for you.

Chapter - 2
Growing from missteps

POV: - *Have you ever made a mistake, whether big, small, or seemingly insignificant? I think we all have. It's completely normal. What truly matters is our mindset toward those mistakes. The past is unchangeable, but with the right mindset, we can learn from our missteps and move forward in a better direction.*

We've all made plenty of mistakes. If you're a student, maybe you've made a misstep in your career planning—or perhaps with your girlfriend or your boyfriend, if you have one (just kidding!). If you're an adult, you've likely made mistakes with financial planning, relationships, jobs, or even in business. It's all part of life. Many people dwell on their mistakes thinking, "What have I done?" or "What will others think?" I've had those thoughts too whenever I've made a mistake. But is sitting in guilt the right way to approach our errors?

We'll be understanding here that "Mistakes" are not failures—they're opportunities for growth and self-improvement. This approach makes us more resilient, adaptable, and successful.

Now, let's explore how you've perceived mistakes until now and what new insights this chapter can offer.

THE MISTAKES - OUR DESTRUCTOR OR OUR FRIEND?

How do you view your mistakes—are they obstacles or allies? Think of mistakes as a coin with two sides. On one side, they can seem like setbacks but if you look at the other side, they can be incredibly valuable.

Many people say, "I worked so hard, yet I didn't pass the exam," or "Despite all my effort, my business failed." Others struggle to manage relationships and start to see themselves as failures. It's easy to think about giving up, whether it's on an exam, a business venture, or a relationship. But is giving up really the right choice?

MISTAKES & SETBACKS

Mistakes and setbacks can feel discouraging, but they also offer valuable lessons. They show us where we might be falling short, why our performance didn't meet our expectations, or why our efforts didn't yield the results we hoped for.

Instead of seeing these experiences as failures, we need to view them as opportunities for growth. It can guide us, helping us understand what went wrong and what to avoid in the future. It's important to recognize when a particular path might not align with your strengths or potential. Ofcourse, there comes a time when you might realize that your potential lies more in something else. If you find that your skills and efforts could be better applied to something else, it's okay to pivot. However, giving up should not be the first option.

ARE MISTAKES BAD?

Our mistakes are not inherently bad until we do them knowingly. Important factors that matter are how we put our thoughts into them, how we view them, and how we respond to them. Tell me, my friend, do you ever let yourself truly feel the emotions that come with making a mistake?

Have you ever taken the time to really experience the moment that taught you something important, something that guides you through tough times?

Listen, we've two types of mindsets when it comes to mistakes. One type sees mistakes negatively and feels bad about them, dwelling on them in a negative manner. The other type views mistakes as valuable lessons, and opportunities to learn something new and grow. We have the choice to decide how we interpret and learn from our mistakes, turning them into chances for growth and improvement.

We have to understand that we are normal human beings and making mistakes is not abnormal for us from any perspective. It is very common to make mistakes but we have to take our minds and our efforts to the best to fix the problem that has arisen from that mistake. We have to edit, retouch, apologize, or do whatever we can do for its rectification. We should never be in any kind of guilt or regret. Instead, we need to take steps to apologize and do whatever we can to make things better.

By making mistakes, we learn what truly matters—what we value, what we want and don't want, what we need and don't need. When we shift our mindset to view mistakes positively, we realize they aren't really bad for our lives. They're lessons and opportunities for growth that life offers us, and not everyone gets such chances.

It's not to bring us down; Mistakes show us what doesn't work and push us to think and act in new, better ways.

THE JOURNEY AND OUR MISTAKES

As they say, if a flower falls from a plant before blooming, it doesn't mean the whole plant is ruined. In the same way, our mistakes are just a part of our journey. If we make a mistake, it doesn't mean we should stop trying new things or hold ourselves back out of fear. "Always remember, a wasted flower is just one part of the plant—it can regrow if nurtured properly". Similarly, with the right mindset and effort, we can bounce back from our mistakes and continue to grow.

When we make mistakes, we become more creative. When we see them as chances to learn, they push us to think differently and find better solutions. This change in how we view mistakes helps us stay positive and find creative ways to solve problems.

When we make a mistake, we often think about why it happened, where we went wrong, and what we missed. We also think about how we can do better in the next try. This process helps us become better thinkers and doers, giving us new ideas and motivating us to move forward with even more energy and determination.

When we set out to do something and fail, we often see it as a mistake. Similarly, if we love someone deeply and the relationship doesn't work out, we might blame ourselves, and our destiny or even sometimes start blaming each other. We face many such situations in life that we see as mistakes, but they're actually valuable lessons. These experiences help us understand our potential and learn how to handle challenges that deeply affect us.

"Remember, if you are not making mistakes, then you are either a god, the creator, or simply not striving hard enough for what you have envisioned in life."

TAKE THE RESPONSIBILITY

We always try to show fake perfection, show off ourselves, and hide mistakes from the outer world. But mistakes aren't the problem; not accepting them is one. When we blame others instead of owning up, we don't learn from what went wrong. This habit of blaming others keeps us from realizing that yes, I've made a mistake and I've to correct it.

There is literally no one who exists in this world who has never made any mistakes, but that doesn't mean they have to pay for the rest of their lives in guilt or regret for that. Sometimes good people also make bad choices and that doesn't mean they are bad. It means they are normal human beings who are trying for something better and have all the right to make mistakes, rectify them, and learn from them.

We should all remember that life's most valuable lessons often come from our toughest times and biggest mistakes. Sometimes, people walk away when we make mistakes, and that's okay. Why? Because those who can't stand by you during your worst moments don't deserve to share in your best ones.

Sometimes, we make a mistake and start treating ourselves like we've done something unforgivable. We focus so much on it that we end up ruining our future too, and that just doesn't make sense. Holding on to the past only leads to more pain, almost like making a new mistake on top of the old one, giving life more power to hurt us. Instead, we should learn to forgive ourselves, learn from what we have faced or facing in the present, fix what we can, and then move on. Don't let one mistake take over your whole life.

TYPES OF MISTAKES

There are two kinds of mistakes: those we *make knowingly* and those we *make unknowingly*, and there's a big difference between them.

<u>Knowing mistakes</u>: - It is when we do something wrong on purpose, fully aware of the possible consequences. This is not justifiable, and it's something we must correct. We have to understand that acting with bad intentions will come back to us as karma has its way of balancing things.

<u>Unknowing mistakes</u>: -The second type of mistake happens unknowingly. While it may still have negative effects, it's more understandable. These mistakes offer valuable lessons—they push us to learn, think creatively, and adjust our perceptions. They remind us that even when things go wrong, there's always something to gain, a new way to grow.

<u>Here's a to-do list for readers after learning from the chapter "Growing from Missteps"</u>:

1. <u>Reflect on past mistakes</u>: Identify what went wrong and what you learned from the experience.

2. <u>Take responsibility</u>: Making mistakes isn't a big deal; everyone makes them. What truly matters is whether

we take responsibility and acknowledge our mistakes or not.

3. <u>Develop an improvement plan</u>: Develop a plan for how to improve and avoid similar missteps in the future.

4. <u>Seek feedback</u>: Embrace criticism as valuable feedback and use it as an opportunity for growth.

5. <u>Practice self-compassion</u>: Be kind and compassionate to yourself as you learn and grow from your mistakes. Remember, mistakes are a natural part of the learning process.

This to-do list helps you use the lessons from "Growing from Missteps" to develop a growth mindset, take responsibility for mistakes and turn them into learning opportunities.

Hoping for a plan of action from you!

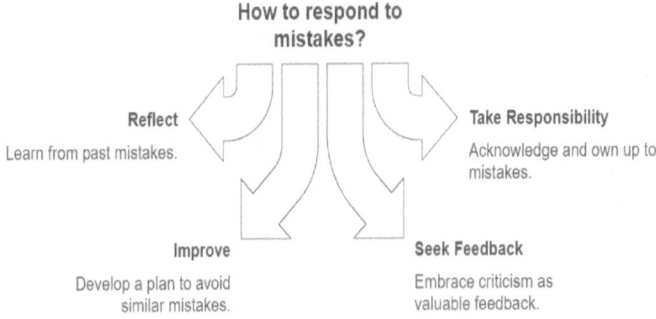

LESSON: - "Mistakes are forgivable because they show you're trying."

Chapter - 3
Self-confidence

POV: - Self-confidence is an essential ingredient for success and happiness in life. It's about believing in yourself and your ability to reach your goals. By practicing self-care, speaking kindly to yourself, and setting realistic goals, you can strengthen your self-confidence and push past self-doubt. Surrounding yourself with supportive people, taking risks, and viewing failures as learning opportunities also help build and sustain confidence. With self-confidence, you're better equipped to overcome challenges and achieve your dreams, leading to a more fulfilling life.

WHAT IS SELF-CONFIDENCE?

In this generation, so many people are left with unfulfilled outcomes and a lack of achievements, and the reason is not the lack of intelligence, opportunities, or resources but a lack of belief and a lack of self-confidence that brings them into this condition.

Self-confidence is a powerful tool that motivates us to strive for more. It helps push our limits and fosters a strong belief in our abilities. Without self-confidence, we put a limit to our potential. But with self-confidence, we can achieve anything we set our minds to, no matter the challenges ahead.

IS IT REALLY A MAGIC?

Some people believe self-confidence is a rare, magical quality that only a few are born with, leaving others wishing they had it. But that's not the case. Self-confidence isn't something you're born with; it's a skill and is built by how you think and the actions you take.

OUR BELIEFS

In a way, we can consider self-confidence as the belief in our ability to speak in front of an audience, take on new challenges, or lead a team. It has the power to shape the course of your life. While it can fluctuate over time, it's important to remember that confidence isn't fixed—it can be rebuilt and strengthened, especially during moments of success.

Sometimes it takes a hit when our efforts fall short of the mark when we get a rejection, when someone criticizes us or it can happen too when we rush into the public without any external recognition.

We must realize that we're humans after all and we have to move out from becoming overly reliant on external affirmations for our self-growth. <u>We must bring a mindset independent from external factors to take the relevant actions needed to sustain in this era.</u>

<u>One of the greatest ways of gaining confidence is by believing in yourself and pretending you already have it.</u> Until you don't speak up for yourself, you don't reach out of your comfort zone, until you don't stretch yourself to do something more extensive, something more significant, you will not be able to accomplish your aim nor you gain that confidence you need to achieve what you aimed for. By doing so, you'll feel a drastic change not only in achieving goals but also gain the confidence you need to succeed.

OVERCONFIDENCE

Sometimes in life when we win anything whether it's about passing an exam, winning a race, winning the lottery, or it's about getting the biggest project in our business, we develop an over-confidence in ourselves, and the time when we lose something we start losing our hopes and this is what we are doing in our life in terms of building and losing faith in a wrong way and it put a result in front of us in losing our confidence and finally, it starts converting into depression and anxiety.

Life is not a problem and we should not waste our time in search of a solution for it. Instead, it should be taken as a game where some rules have already been made and we have to play the game by considering the rules that comply here.

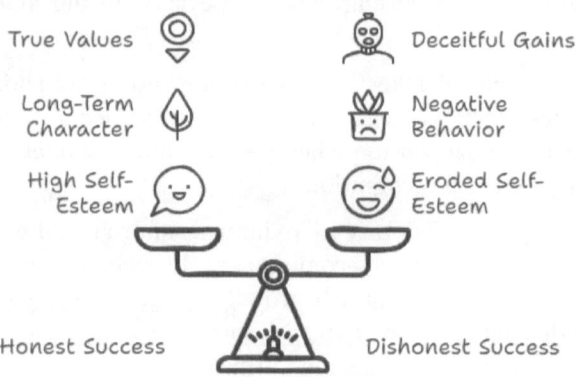

Honest efforts lead to lasting self-esteem and character.

There are two types of people:

PERSON A: The one who is playing with proper rules ethically but even after playing the game with honesty, if he loses the game, his self-esteem remains high because he knows he gave his best efforts and stayed true to the values. He became responsible without breaking any rules.

PERSON B: The one who focuses only on winning by disregarding the rules. While he might achieve success, he does so dishonestly, which ultimately erodes his self-esteem. Winning through deceit may bring short-term gains, but it fosters a habit of negative behavior that undermines their character in the long run. This highlights the clear difference between an honest and a dishonest person.

OUR PERCEPTION!

Do you know what kind of wrong perception we are developing in our lives? We are just loving the results, we love to see people clapping for us but when we talk about the hard work and the sacrifices we lose ourselves there. It's like we want to be on the top but hate to work with sincerity, it's like we want to see our bank balance full of money but hate to work hard for it and this is what needs to be corrected the most in today's generation's mindsets.

Everyone has something they're passionate about, but instead of just aiming to win, they should focus on enjoying the journey. When they care more about playing their best than just winning, they'll end up getting the results they deserve.

THE ROLE OF A MENTOR

Once, a celebrated author Bob Proctor so candidly said: ***"A mentor is someone who sees more talent and ability within you, than you see in yourself, and helps bring it out of you."*** We all need a mentor in our lives: someone who can gently help us when we go off the track, guide us and show us what to do, and lift us during down times. Life is full of small challenges and it has the power to either boost our confidence or break it. If we want to harness that power, we shouldn't focus solely on the outcome; instead, we should keep our attention on the game we're playing.

Just like plants need someone to care for them, we also need someone to nurture and guide us. Without a mentor, every turn in life can become more difficult.

CHOOSING THE RIGHT MENTOR

However, be mindful of who you choose as your mentor. Taking advice from someone who doesn't truly understand what you're trying to achieve can be more harmful than having no mentor at all. It's like taking cricket tips from someone who's never played, trying to teach you how to hit a helicopter shot. So, think carefully about who your mentor could be—It must be someone who knows the field and can genuinely help you grow.

Just like in life, if you want to learn how to cook great food, you should seek out a master chef. If you want to excel in football, you should go to a coach. If you want to learn acting, you should learn from an actor, and if your dream is to become a doctor, you need to take advice from the person who's a doctor. You wouldn't go to a Sanskrit teacher to learn English, right?

Think about it this way: when you want a beautiful art showcasing your home, you seek an artist; when you want to build a house, you go to an architect; when you want sweets, you go to a specific sweet shop. We do this because we understand where to find what we need. Now, if you accidentally go to the wrong shop there's a chance for correction, but if you once choose the wrong mentor or guide in life, it can lead to disastrous consequences.

That's why it's so important to understand the value of having the right mentor. If you haven't figured out who can guide you correctly, take the time to find the right person. Choosing the wrong guide can derail your life, just like trying to learn English from a Sanskrit teacher. So, think carefully about who can truly help you move forward and make sure you seek out the right guidance for your goals.

SELF-CONFIDENCE or OVER-CONFIDENCE

When someone is new to a field and doesn't seek guidance from experts, it's often not true self-confidence but rather over-confidence. On the other hand, a person at the same level who asks experts for help and is eager to learn more shows genuine self-confidence. They understand that guidance is valuable for doing things right.

Be informed that everything we do will yield results, whether it's success or failure. Both outcomes teach us important lessons. Success motivates us to aim higher, while failure teaches us what to avoid in the future.

Also, remember that everyone has 24 hours in a day, but how we use that time makes the difference. If you plan to complete 8 tasks but manage to finish 10 with greater energy and productivity, you'll feel a unique sense of achievement. To make your day more fulfilling, include something you enjoy as a reward for going above and beyond. Nothing compares to the satisfaction of achieving more than you planned for in your day.

A "To do list" based on the learnings about Self-Confidence:

1. _Spot your Superpowers_: Reflect on your unique skills, talents, and abilities. What are you great at? Celebrate those strengths.

2. _Set realistic Goals:_ Set achievable goals aligning with your passion.

3. _Practice Positive Self-talk:_ Use positive affirmations to boost your self-confidence. Remind yourself of your strengths.

4. _Build a Positive Squad:_ Surround yourself with visionaries who help you to grow.

5. _Take the leap:_ Push yourself out of your comfort zone and take action. As 'A single move – can make a change.'

By following this to-do list, you'll harness the power of self-confidence to boost your productivity and achieve your goals.

Building Self-Confidence

LESSON:- *No one can make you feel inferior unless you allow them. When you recognize your own potential and build your self-confidence, you'll be able to create a better life for yourself.*

Chapter - 4
Do we bounce back after failures?

POV:- Failures are a natural part of life, and how we respond to them, really matters. Instead of dwelling on mistakes, focus on the lessons they teach you and use that knowledge to move forward. Be kind to yourself—everyone fails sometimes. Build resilience by surrounding yourself with supportive people, taking care of yourself, and staying committed to your goals. What counts is not how many times you fall, but how often you get up and bounce back.

WHAT IS FAILURE?

Failure—yes, I'm talking about failure. Can you please tell me what failure means as per your definition? Is it when you fail an exam? Is it about failing to achieve something on the first try? I think our understanding of failure is not practical. We often think that when we prepare for something and succeed, we achieve success and if we fall short, we call ourselves failures. People say, "Prepare to win." No, I think there is a win in our preparation. "*Taiyari jeet ki nahi, taiyari mein jeet honi chahiye.*" It's important to remember that if we've given our best effort, we don't deserve to be labeled as failures. Consider a group of soldiers who march towards their targets—they may become martyrs or fall short, but they never give up, never take back their step of actions. This mindset helps distinguish between merely failing and being a true warrior.

CONTRIBUTIONS OF UNSUCCESSFUL RESULTS!

Let's talk about the contributions of some unsuccessful results impacting our lives. No one enjoys the thought of being unsuccessful, and I'm no exception. While writing this book, I'm also having some doubts—wondering if I'll be able to finish it, find a good publisher, or if my research and insights into teenage and bachelor experiences will truly address your challenges. I've also worried about whether readers will relate to my writing and feel the connection. But these doubts are completely normal. Without the fear of failure, we might not take our work or our tasks as seriously as we should. So, it's good if you have a fear of failing in your task.

HATE TO BE UNSUCCESSFUL?

Do you know why we hate to be unsuccessful? Do you know who is the real master of life? Is that someone who solves all of their problems or someone who is always positive and ready to fight their problems? Who? In reality, the definition of the same is different for everyone. Everyone might have a different meaning, their followings, their approach. But in reality, if we try to look deeper, then the person who has conquered their mind is the real achiever. It's because your thoughts, your feelings, and your emotions that are controlling your life are also controlling your actions towards it and accordingly you get the results. When you start thinking deeply about whether your thoughts are correct to be on the top or not, your perception about it might start changing and when your perception starts changing, your actions start moving in another direction and when your actions start moving into the direction, your outcome will automatically change. This is the only way to understand the path to success instead of facing failures.

Everything in life contributes to our growth, whether it's positive or negative. If we want to rise above challenges, we first need to develop our mindset, emotions, and perspective to go beyond our current limits.

Let me give you an example: Imagine a person flying from New York to Chicago. As he approaches the airport, he sees a tall building and has to tilt his head up, amazed by its height. But once his plane takes off and reaches the sky, that same building disappears from view.

The lesson here is simple: when we view something from a limited perspective, it can seem overwhelming, like a huge obstacle in our lives. But as we grow and elevate our thinking, that same problem becomes insignificant, just like the building from the plane. So, when facing tough times, it's important to find solutions and not dwell on the problem itself.

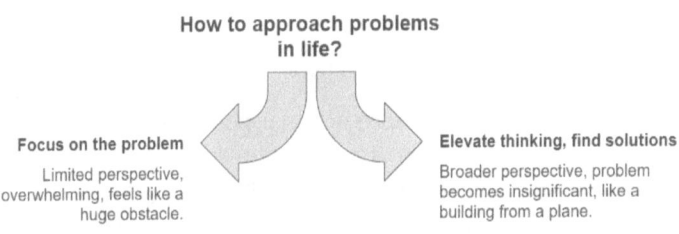

THE BOUNCEBACK:

Bounceback is a thrill that recharges our mind to stand out once again in a more energetic way, in a more synthetic manner.

Ever you look at the group of ants, if you ever observed them you can possibly analyze what they do when they fall. They never leave their way, they never get demotivated by falling, they never criticize someone for their screw-up, they just stand up again and bounce back with a new energetic thrill and if some of them felt difficult to move out further after falling, the whole group comes along as a support to make that ant take a successful stand to move again with a little more motivation. And this is what we people need to understand and take as a lesson for us. It's because no one exists with highness for the whole of their lives nor does anyone exist with a permanent downfall, it's just a matter of concern, helping nature and the supporting mindsets that we have for others.

Guys, do you know what is the most important thing other than a mentor in one's life that keeps the power to make a difference between success and failure?

The answer is - 'A Backup.' No no no I didn't mean about any alternatives. I mean 'a genuine support.' It can be either any person who makes us feel like a support system and encourages us to do more. That can be your father, your mother, your friends, your mentor, your girlfriend, your boyfriend, your life partner, or anyone who can make you feel that support or there can be any materialistic things like the dream of buying your own house, buying a luxury car for your dad or anything else.

Are you thinking you're not in a position to dream so big? In reality, nothing matters whatever happens in your life. Whatever the level you are in, or how badly you have failed, but that one person who motivates you and is always with you, who's your inspiration will always be there to put his shoulder for you whenever you need them the most. And this works as a PowerPoint for us, this gives us the motivation to do more and to perform better which results in growth from every perspective. People fail, in everyone's life there is a failure, some face it in their relationships, someone in their businesses, and someone in their health but it doesn't matter how badly you fall, what matters is how high you bounce back from it, and this will decide the turning point of your life.

HOW OUR MINDS WORK

Now let me tell you a story about a person who is full of experience and talent, who is not less than a glamorous individual, I'm talking about a plot character named Mr. R.K. Beniwal, he is a businessman who runs a million-dollar company but a turning point in his life dwells him into a huge amount of debt and was unable to see a way out of the mess. The accounts are going to settle down and the company is going to move almost into a phase of bankruptcy. He was unable to find a way to tackle those situations, one day he went around a park and sat on a bench under a tree holding his head in his hands, wondering if there could be a way that could save his company from closing down. He had given his best and tried everything possible, but nothing worked.

As the man sat there ridden with worries, an old man came and sat right next to him. The old man said, "You are looking so disturbed." Is there anything I can do for you? Please tell me what has happened. At first, he replied nervously, saying to the old man, "You wouldn't understand, just forget it." But when the old man gently reassured him, saying, "I know you're really worried, but don't stress. I'm like your father—please, tell me what's bothering you." Then the man opened his mind and said everything to that old man and it made him feel better and lighter as if he was holding a huge trauma and now he had someone with whom he shared everything, the businessman told him all his problems. After listening to the executive's story the old man said, "He can help him."

He asked the man his name and wrote out a cheque, and gave it to him saying, take this money and meet me back exactly after 10 months at the same place and you can pay me back at that time. After saying this the old man disappeared quickly. The businessman was astonished by what he saw, it was a million dollars cheque signed by one of the richest men in the country, Mr. John S Parker. The businessman was astonished and had a smile on his face, as he knew that with this uncashed cheque, he would be able to save his company from bankruptcy. But instead of using that cheque right away, he decided to put it in his safe.

Now he could still give another shot to save his company without using that cheque. After all, if nothing worked, he had a million-dollar cheque as a security to his fallback option to salvage his business from bankruptcy. With renewed optimism, the businessman negotiated better deals and extended his terms of payment.

He is now performing better and also closed multiple big sales and within a few months he became a debt-free person without using a single penny from the cheque that he had gotten from the old man and his business restarted to make money. Now exactly 10 months later, he returned to that park as per the contract with the uncashed cheque in his hand. As agreed upon at the time the old man also appeared. He is now about to share his success story and hand over the uncashed cheque when a lady comes running and holds the old man into her arms.

She said I'm glad I caught you and started crying. 'I hope he is not bothering you,' she said to Mr. Beniwal, the businessman. He is always escaping the home and telling people that he is Mr. John S Parker. And then she walked away with the old man. The astonished businessman just stood there. All time long he has been dealing, buying, and selling with the confidence that he had a million-dollar cheque with him. Suddenly he realized that it is not the money that turned his life around, it was his newly found self-confidence, the courage that had given him the power to achieve anything in life even at his downfall. The old man himself was not John S Parker. So, we should understand that when we go through massive challenges in our lives, we can end up feeling anxious and helpless. Sometimes, to the extent of wanting to end our lives, we feel drained.

You know what we need to fight with a challenge? It's not the resources, but the confidence and the strength to fight it out and that's what we badly lack at that time when we have some difficulties behind us, that support can help us pull through all the difficulties and bounce back to success with gratitude and wisdom. So, guys do you have your Mr. John S Parker?

If not then search for the one because it's good to have a real one around so that you can also bounce back to the difficult phases of your lives, if needed.

Always be mindful that wherever you fall, the comeback will always be stronger than the setback and that should be the main reason for your turn-around. Take your time, recharge yourself, and come again with a thrill of bounce back. You are strong, always remember that!

Here's a to-do list after harnessing the concept of "Do we bounce back after failures":

1. Accept failure: Failure is a natural part of life and everyone experiences it at some point. Accepting it will help move on and bounce back.

2. Reframe your mindset: Develop a growth mindset and see failures as opportunities to learn and grow, rather than something to be ashamed of.

3. Analyze the failure: Take your time to reflect on what went wrong and why. Analyze the failure to identify areas for improvement and how to avoid similar mistakes in the future.

4. Seek support: Reach out to friends, families, or a professional for support and guidance. Having a support system can help you bounce back more easily.

5. Take action: Take action towards the goal, even if you feel afraid or uncertain. Take small steps and focus on progress, not perfection.

By following this to-do list, you can cultivate resilience and move forward after experiencing setbacks.

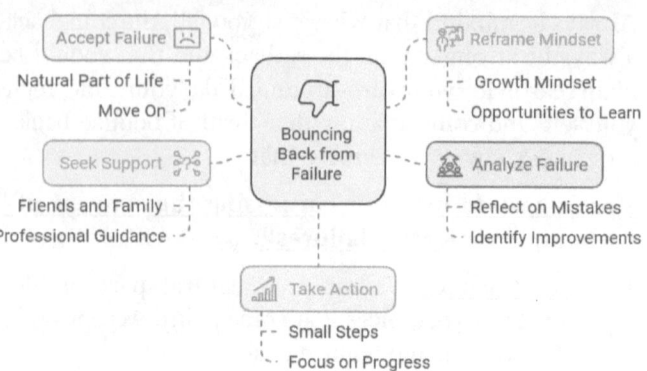

<u>**LESSON**</u>:- Genuine support and courage to bounce back can transform you from a failure to a successor.

Chapter - 5
Fear of trying something new

POV:- Has fear ever stopped you from moving ahead with your goals? If your answer is yes, then this chapter is for you. You know how sometimes your mind starts to wander into thoughts of fear of failing when you go to take on something new, like a new class you are going to sign up for, studying for that exam, or right before that new business idea you're about to take a plunge with? The chapter "Fear of Trying Something New" gives you the "how-to" phenomenon to get beyond those fears and take the risks required to chase your goals.

Have you ever felt fear before getting yourself into some unfamiliar stuff? Imagine you're an introvert and today you have to perform in front of a large crowd—there's no other option. What thoughts immediately flood your mind? Will you be able to push past your fear and give your best?

As humans, we all share common emotions, and one of them is fear. Fear often arises when we think about trying something new, whether starting a different career, a new job, a business venture or even navigating relationships. The reason we fear stepping into the unknown is that, when it's time to act, our minds tend to focus on all the possible ways we might fail, or we start worrying too much about the future instead of focusing on the process and it's very common between all of us. But do we really understand what we are fearful of? Why do we get these kinds of emotions while starting something new or going to attempt an exam in which we know that the passing percentage is unfortunately very low? Let's try to understand the phenomena.

WHAT MAKES US FEARFUL ACTUALLY?

Have you ever considered the impact of fear that holds you back from pursuing what you truly want to achieve? It's like a paralyzing emotion that can freeze our minds, stopping us from taking on new challenges because we fear the possibility of failure. It can be seen in multiple manners, there are two types of people: those who don't move forward with their actions due to this fearful emotion of failing, and the second one are those who act more generously, more sincerely because they know that if their actions don't bring the sincerity on the table, they can fail.

I think we generally focus more on getting a better result instead of enjoying the process. Once in a research study, two groups were assigned the same task to complete in 15 days. Group A was told they would receive a 100% salary hike if they outperformed Group B, while Group B wasn't informed of any reward, just that the task was important.

Surprisingly, Group B delivered better results. When asked why, Group A revealed they kept thinking about the competition and the reward, which caused them to constantly second-guess and revise their work. This led to distractions and inefficiency. Group B, on the other hand, simply focused on enjoying the process and delivering the task without any pressure of rewards. They stayed in the moment and performed better.

This teaches us an important lesson: when we focus too much on the end results or rewards, it can create anxiety and affect our performance. But if we concentrate on the process and enjoy the journey, better results come naturally.

Fear can be sometimes helpful too.

For example, if you're an ordinary person and someone challenges you to a fistfight with a trained boxer, feeling fearful is natural and can actually protect you from making a dangerous decision. In moments like these, fear can be a valuable instinct that helps you avoid serious consequences.

Now the questions are:-

- Why do we panic when we try something new?
- Why does our mind interrupt as if it has some dangerous element?
- Did you ever feel embarrassed after a failure when you tried something different, something new?
- Does learning something new or doing something different remind you of a person from whom your mind is preparing to protect you?

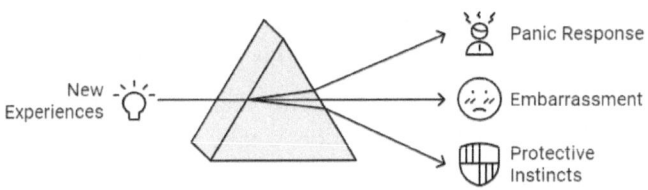

I think we can relate to these few points why we feel fear when we think of being involved in something new, something unfavorable to our personalities.

If you could identify the root cause of your fear, you could make yourself feel safer and your brain would learn to stop triggering that protective emotion.

There are mainly two things that often hold us back from exploring new and unfamiliar areas or having different life experiences:

First:- "The fear of stepping out of our comfort zone" and

Second:- "The fear of being judged by others or society."

You know, the biggest difference between a child and an adult is that children love challenges and adventures. But as we grow up as adults, we often stick to our comfort zones instead of trying something new. And do you know why this happens?

Child   **Adult**

Loves challenges   Sticks to comfort

Remember when we were little kids? Back then, we didn't enjoy relaxing or sleeping as much as we enjoyed doing challenging things. I'm sure you've also done something in your childhood that was a bit challenging for you. And have you ever tried observing why this is happening?

As we grow older, we face many challenges that gradually suppress our inner child. This is why we start to shy away from new experiences. Over time success, fame, and financial security become more important to us than creativity. We begin to prioritize what society expects from us over our own happiness. This often leads us to fall into a routine, living a life that seems robotic, just to fit into societal norms and earn respect. And when we follow that path, we start blaming our destiny for our dissatisfaction.

Society has shaped our mindset in such a way that even many parents start imposing similar expectations on their children. For instance, if the neighbor's son becomes a successful doctor, your parents and neighbors might push you to follow the same path without considering what you truly want from life. If someone wants to start a business, they might be advised to stick with a stable job instead, without understanding the child's passion and desires.

But sooner or later, we all need to realize some important things that can help us achieve what we truly want in life. For example, stepping out of your comfort zone and trying something new can reveal hidden strengths and abilities you never knew you had. The challenges of new tasks force you to think more, research more, and ultimately, boost your self-confidence.

A few years ago, I never imagined I would be writing a book or that I would become an author with my own published work. But as time went on, I discovered a deep interest in researching and understanding the human mind. When I looked at myself and observed the struggles of today's teenagers and bachelors, I began to understand the challenges our generation is facing—how we handle different situations and why so many of today's youth end up stuck in a trap, falling behind.

Every innovation and innovator starts by trying something new, something different that signifies them an "innovator", and who knows you would be the next. It can only take some of your time, I think everyone should try something new at least once in their lifetime. Giving a thought about getting success or failure is the next thing but at least trying out something new doesn't make you lose anything. Trying out unfamiliar stuff makes you courageous to take new steps in life. Once your mind adapts to get into things, you will never get yourself down by fear of failure or getting into anything new. This will be your biggest success that you have been moving out from the fear of what society would say if you do something different. And this is the way that can help you create a different, better personality for yourself. People generally plan to take up new things as a New Year's resolution, it's alright but why should we have to wait till the end of the existing year to initiate something new, why can't we start right now?

If you think you have an ideologist mind then why should you wait to start another year for that, why not from today you can plan to initiate your ideas that you are thinking to initiate as a new year's resolution.

If you've decided to overcome your fear as a staircase, then you've to take one step at a time. ***If you try to jump, your chances of falling increases.*** And no matter what new skill it is that you're trying to pick up, you probably won't have a boom at the beginning, but if you are planning to learn and experience something new, then I must say it'll be the most adorable decision you have made for yourself. It doesn't matter what people comment on you while you're doing your work. If your performance is beyond level, you can make history.

People tend to get themselves into a new skill in two ways, some approach new things just to seek knowledge, while others want to master it. If we don't think about failures before starting something, no one can stop us from achieving our full potential.

One of the reasons why new things seem scary for us is either it is unfamiliar to us or we are going to do it for the first time.

<u>The fear of trying new things is often called neophobia.</u> Especially in cases where the fear is persistent. And the best thing about this emotion is that we can overcome it, and the bad news is that the only way to overcome it is to go straight through it.

The best way to conquer any fear is to start small and work on your way to the bigger and really scary stuff. Let me give you an example: if you want to become a bestselling author and you are afraid of thinking whether your book will be interesting or not, then you can first start by writing small articles and you can send your write-ups to the person who is an inspiration to you or you can show it to the people around you. It's because if you're afraid of taking risks then it would be good to analyze the group of audience that you think would be interested in your stuff. It is sometimes essential to collect some positive experiences and little success that can help you to move forward.

Millions of people suppress their wishes and ruin their dreams just by thinking about the end results and the comments of the people on it, but not all. And you have to decide whether you'll disappear with your dream among these millions of people or you'll be the one who steps differently and be different to make your position out of this population.

Most of the time we get scared if the condition demands a drop-down after starting a new thing and it is normal to happen because when we start something, we create a scenario in our mind for the level of the outcome from our goals. At that time, take a moment to figure out what we can control about the situation. Fear is as normal as breathing, where new means uncertainty and uncertainty causes anxiety, and if you can think of it differently you can bring out an ability to achieve different results.

Now I think if you understand the part, you'll not be afraid to take the first step to anything with a message to your mind that every new beginning is the end of another one. So, stop being afraid of what can be wrong and just be excited about what would be the boom and how amazing your journey will be.

<u>Here's a to-do list based on the learnings from the chapter "Fear of Trying Something New":</u>

1. <u>Identify your fears</u>: Take time to identify what is holding you back from trying something new. Is it fear of failure, fear of the unknown, or something else?

2. <u>Reframe your mindset</u>: Shift your mindset from fear to curiosity and growth. Try seeing new things as an opportunity to learn and grow, rather than something to be afraid of. Don't quit right after a trial.

3. <u>Take small steps</u>: Start with small, manageable steps towards trying new things. This will therefore help you achieve momentum and confidence.

4. <u>Build a support system</u>: Surround yourself with people who encourage and believe in you to try new things. Always remember - Negative people suck the energy within us.

5. <u>Celebrate your success</u>: Celebrate the tiniest success you achieve, even though it's completing a chapter or a small work. When you celebrate for yourself - You feel better.

LESSON:- *You never know what is your potential, or what can be the outcome until you give it a try. So, do not let your fear stop you from achieving what you have dreamt of. Today make a promise to yourself that you'll not let anything stop you from evolving.*

Chapter - 6
Our purposeful goals

POV:- The chapter "Our Purposeful Goals" explores the concept of setting goals that are aligned with our values and desires. Readers will learn that having purposeful goals can give direction and meaning to their lives, and help them stay motivated and focused.

The chapter will delve into the process of setting purposeful goals, including identifying core values, envisioning the desired outcome, and creating an action plan. It will also explore the importance of resilience and adaptability in the pursuit of our goals. Through this chapter, readers will be empowered to set and pursue purposeful goals that align with their values and bring fulfillment to their lives. They will gain the confidence and tools to overcome obstacles and achieve their dreams.

Do you understand the significance of having goals in your life? For some, goals may be short-term tasks, while for others, they represent long-term achievements.

THE FOUR 1s

Before diving into this chapter, take a notebook and divide it into four columns labeled 1D (One Day), 1W (One Week), 1M (One Month), and 1Y (One Year). Now, you might be wondering what I'm aiming to illustrate here.

Each day, we face numerous tasks, and they all contribute to our broader objectives. For instance, imagine being told to prepare for an IIT exam. For many, this might create a sense of discomfort. It's normal because larger goals can feel overwhelming and mentally burdensome. This is why it's crucial to develop the skill of breaking our life and goals into manageable parts.

Everyone has big dreams—becoming a Doctor, a Chartered Accountant, or an IAS officer. But unless we break these goals into smaller, actionable steps, achieving them becomes challenging.

Think about how you approach a book. Typically, you glance at the contents or synopsis first. Then, you might notice that each chapter contains approximately 10 pages of content, and then you decide to finish the one today. Similarly, when we break down a year-long goal into monthly milestones, it feels lighter. Breaking a month into weeks and a week into days makes the task more manageable. We need to break down goals according to our capabilities.

When we focus on the day's task rather than the ultimate goal, it allows us to move more concisely and productively. This method is the key to tackling large, seemingly overwhelming goals—like eating an elephant one bite each day to finish it in a year. By focusing on just one task per day, the fear associated with tackling huge goals disappears, allowing our days to flow with increased productivity and ease.

HOW PURPOSEFUL?

In today's time, setting goals is a crucial step toward achieving success, happiness, and personal fulfillment.

However, not all goals are created equal. To truly realize our potential, it's important to set purposeful goals - ones that align with our values, beliefs, and aspirations. In this chapter, we'll explore the concept of purposeful goals, why they matter, and how to set them effectively.

Do you know what are our Purposeful Goals?

Why I added the word purposeful to the heading?

Purposeful goals are those that are deeply connected to our sense of purpose, meaning, and fulfillment. They are the goals that are based on our passions, values, and unique strengths, rather than external pressures or expectations. It reflects our innermost desires and aspirations and gives us a sense of direction that makes our lives more meaningful.

Why do Purposeful Goals Matter?

Setting purposeful goals can have a profound impact on our lives. Here I've tried to put some reasons why it matters:

<u>Increased Motivation</u>: When we set purposeful goals, we're more likely to be motivated to achieve them. Because these goals are aligned with our values and passions, they're inherently more meaningful and fulfilling.

<u>Greater Clarity and Direction</u>: Purposeful goals give us a clear sense of direction and help us focus our efforts. They provide a roadmap for where we want to go in life and how we want to get there.

<u>Improved Well-Being</u>: Moving with a purposeful goal can improve our overall well-being and happiness. Studies have shown that people who pursue goals that are aligned with their values and passions experience higher levels of satisfaction and fulfillment in life.

How to Set Purposeful Goals?

Now we've acknowledged why purposeful goals matter, let's explore how to set them effectively.

Here are some practical ways to maintain discipline with determination to achieve what you plan:

1. <u>Identify Your Values:</u> The first step in setting purposeful goals is to identify your values. What matters most to you? What do you want your life to be about? Reflect on your core beliefs and principles to identify the values that are most important to you.

2. <u>Consider Your Passions</u>: Next, think about your passion and interest. What do you love doing? What activities bring you the most joy and fulfillment? Consider how you can align your passions with your values.

3. <u>Assess Your Strengths</u>: What are your unique strengths and talents? What skills and competencies do you possess that will help you achieve your goals? Identify your strengths and consider how you can leverage them to pursue your purposeful goals.

4. <u>Set Specific, Measurable, Attainable, Relevant, and Time-bound (SMART) Goals</u>: Once you've identified your values, passions, and strengths, it's time to set specific goals that align with these factors. Use the SMART criteria to ensure that your goals are well-defined and achievable.

5. <u>Take Action</u>: Finally, take action towards your purposeful goals. Break them down into smaller, manageable steps, and create a plan to achieve them. Stay motivated and focused, and don't be afraid to adjust your goals as needed.

6. <u>Stay Accountable</u>: Find someone to hold you accountable for your goals. This could be a friend, family member, or even a coach. Regularly share your goals and progress with them, and ask for feedback and support when needed. Knowing that you've to report your track of progress can help keep you motivated and on track.

7. <u>Bring Self-Control</u>: Maintaining discipline requires self-control and consistency. Set specific times for working on your goals and stick to them, even if it means sacrificing other activities. Avoid distractions like social media or Television shows during your dedicated work times.

8. <u>Celebrate Small Wins</u>: Celebrate little victories along the way to keep yourself motivated. Recognize and reward yourself when you achieve a milestone or complete a task. This will help keep you motivated and remind you of the progress you're making toward your purposeful goal.

By implementing these practical tips, you can maintain discipline and determination to achieve what you genuinely plan to have in your life. Remember, success requires effort and commitment, but with a clear purpose and disciplined approach, you can achieve anything you set your mind to.

Let me tell you a simple and process-driven story:

Once upon a time, there was a young woman named Sara. She was divorced having two children. She was the one who was deriving the responsibility of a single parent. She solely committed herself to bringing up both the children with each facility, and for that, she was truly working hard enough. She had always dreamed of becoming a successful entrepreneur and starting her own business but life doesn't give her a chance yet. Sara knew that it wouldn't be easy, but she was determined to pursue her purposeful goal.

One day, Sara decided to attend a business conference in the city. There, she met a successful entrepreneur named Marcus, a hustler, who had a paralyzed body, shared his inspiring story of how he converted his mindset from an introvert to an open-minded person, how he tackled all the situations, from the mindset of having paralyzed body into recognizing the opportunity and analyzing the talent, the ability to move forward, how he unlocked his potential to grow up and turned his purposeful goal into a thriving business. Sara was motivated by Marcus's story and asked him for advice on how to achieve her own purposeful goal.

Marcus advised Sarah to break down her goal into smaller, achievable tasks and to stay disciplined in her efforts. Marcus was an inspiration for Sara so she took his advice to heart and began working hard to make her dream a reality. She spent countless hours researching her industry, networking with other entrepreneurs, and developing her business plan.

Despite facing numerous setbacks and challenges, Sara remained committed to her purposeful goal. She refused to give up and continued pushing forward, one step at a time.

Finally, after months of hard work, Sara's dream became a reality. She launched her own business and found success beyond her wildest dreams. Looking back on her journey, Sarah realized that her purposeful goal had given her direction, focus, and motivation to pursue her passion.

In the end, Sara learned that it doesn't matter in which situation you are in, you can unlock your potential by recognizing the opportunity. She has developed a mindset that by setting a purposeful goal and maintaining discipline, anyone can be able to make the impossible break into "I'm Possible". Her story serves as a reminder that anything is possible with hard work, determination, and a clear sense of purpose.

<u>So, the conclusion is:</u>

Setting purposeful goals can have a transformative impact on our lives. By aligning our goals with our values, passion, and strengths, we can increase our motivation, clarity, and overall well-being. By following the steps outlined in this chapter, you can set purposeful goals that will help you achieve success and fulfillment in all areas of your life.

here's a to-do list that you can consider as key learnings of this chapter "Our Purposeful Goals":

1. Identify your core values: Take time to reflect on what is most important to you in life. This will help you identify goals that are aligned with your values.

2. Envision your desired outcome: Visualize what achieving your goals will look and feel like. This will help you stay motivated and focused.

3. Create a plan of action: Break your goals into actionable steps, and create a timeline for achieving them. This will help you stay organized and accountable.

4. Stay resilient and adaptable: Recognize that setbacks and obstacles are a natural part of the journey toward achieving your goals.

5. Seek support and accountability: Share your goals with trusted friends or family members, or join a group or community focused on similar goals. This will help keep you accountable and motivated.

6. Celebrate your progress: It's so important to take a moment to recognize and celebrate your achievements, even the small ones. Doing this can really uplift your spirits and help you maintain your motivation as you move forward. You deserve to acknowledge your progress!

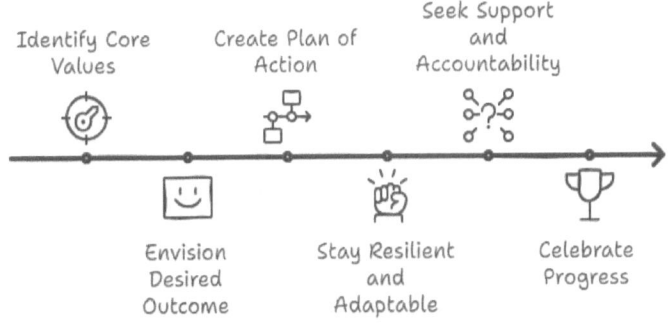

Hey, champ! You're a quarter of the way through this book. Congratulations! Look at what's on your to-do list and decide for yourself whether it is really helping. Implement key rules that align with your goals. Keep moving forward!

LESSON:- It is not your situation that stops you from growing your potential, it is you and your disciplinary mindset that decides whether you grow or freeze the opportunities by closing your eyes at the same level.

Chapter - 7
Embracing imperfection

POV:- This chapter explores how embracing imperfection changes the game. By embracing our own flaws, we grow as people, we learn to accept ourselves, and we build meaningful relationships. Celebrating imperfections leads to satisfaction and shows how beautiful, messy humanity is!

One day I met a person named John, he was a committed and dedicated delivery boy at Zomato, really putting his heart and soul into every single aspect of his job, even if he sometimes committed mistakes as minute as taking the wrong order from a client. He was desired to be perfect in everything to attain mastery in his job. But, instead of getting appreciation from his boss and others at the company, he faced constant criticism, which ultimately pushed John to strive for perfection more relentlessly. Though Driven by the desire to please his boss and meet expectations, John began to work overtime, sometimes neglecting friends and family too; the immense pressure from his job started to take a big toll on his well-being. The job started taking a wrong turn for him, he started overthinking and not being perfect made his mind filled with stress and then he ended up downgrading his performance and getting a letter of warning as a consequence of what he was going through.

One day his friend Rohan ordered something from a restaurant through Zomato and unfortunately John got a notification to deliver the order. So, he picked the order from the restaurant and started moving to reach his friend's home to deliver the order, he seemed happy but immediately he got a call from his manager warning him that if he makes any mistake from now on he'll end up losing his job. John reached his friend's place and rang the bell at the door, Rohan opened the gate for him with a surprising look. Looking at John's face, Rohan immediately understood that something is not good here. And when he asked John what happened, he told him everything and then Rohan just asked a simple question, "Is being perfect really that important?", John sat mulling over what it meant. He realized on sober thought that he was putting tremendous effort into his work but achieving nothing of value in return because he had neglected the core truth behind what success would truly mean. His company valued and appreciated what he was bringing to the table, but this relentless pursuit of perfection started causing a lot of stress and confusion in his mind.

Here we've to understand why "Embracing Imperfection" is important for us. We have to understand that running after perfection can completely divert our attention away from really valuing ourselves and our worth and progress.

After all, in a world in which perfection is desired, in which perfection is the goal, where even tiny mistakes are seen as bad, we need to challenge this way of thinking, and we must move on a journey accepting beauty and strength in those imperfections. In this chapter, we focus our attention on what might be termed the liberating idea of accepting imperfections, and how it can radically change one's life. Now, let us let go of this futile aspiration for perfection and open our hearts and minds to the scope of possibilities within the acceptance of our beautifully imperfect self.

WHY WE FEEL THE URGE TO BE PERFECT?

Do you know most people feel the urge to seem perfect in today's world? The endless hunt for perfection has become an enormous part of our culture, and very little room is left for self-acceptance and personal existence. Yet, many studies show that accepting flaws results in better mental health and a more enjoyable life.

In today's fast-paced world, many people are so filled up with responsibilities that they hardly have time for other stuffs, not even for their family or friends. This continuous stress has made the mental health problems mount in the way of anxiety, panic attacks, heart problems, and suicides. Pursuing the goal of perfection on top of this burden will drive mental well-being further downhill. So, if you are not perfect at something, that's alright; just do your best without damaging your health or your relationships because jobs are replaceable but your health and the relationships with your loved ones are not.

Further study reveals that those embracing their flaws have less stress, greater self-esteem, and stronger relationships with others. So, as we get started with this chapter, let's consider practical ways of embracing imperfections and the great benefits it brings for a happier and more real life.

We all should accept the flaws we've in our lives because it significantly helps in conducting a happier and more real life.

Let's discuss some straightforward strategies and talk about the benefits that they can provide:

A. Practice self-compassion:

- Treat yourself with kindness and understanding when you make mistakes or fall short of your expectations.
- Recognize that imperfections are a natural part of being human, and they don't define your worth.

Benefit: Self-compassion fosters resilience, boosts self-esteem, and reduces stress and anxiety, leading to improved overall well-being.

B. <u>Embrace vulnerability</u>:

The following are the key points to understand for embracing imperfections and being vulnerable:

- **<u>Authenticity</u>**: Accept yourself with all your flaws and strengths, allowing others to see the real you.
- **<u>Vulnerability</u>**: Share your struggles and insecurity with people you trust that engrosses your emotional strength.
- **<u>Support System:</u>** Keep friends/people connected who care and understand you.
- **<u>Deep Connections</u>**: Vulnerability brings about real, deep relationships; other people appreciate honesty and openness.
- **<u>Growth</u>**: Embracing imperfections leads to personal development and stronger bonds with others.

<u>Benefit</u>: By embracing vulnerability, you cultivate stronger, more meaningful connections and foster an environment of trust and understanding in your relationships.

C. <u>Shift perspective:</u>

- Challenge societal norms of perfection and recognize that imperfections are opportunities for growth and learning.
- Reframe mistakes as valuable lessons and view them as stepping stairs toward personal development.

<u>Benefit</u>: Shifting your perspective on imperfections helps you develop a growth mindset, where setbacks are seen as opportunities for growth and self-improvement, fostering resilience and adaptability.

D. Focus on progress, not perfection:

- Instead of pursuing perfection, shift your focus to progress and growth.
- Embrace the journey by setting achievable goals and honoring every small victory along the way.
- Recognize that progress is not always linear and that setbacks and mistakes are part of the journey.

Benefit: By focusing on progress rather than perfection, you develop a sense of accomplishment and motivation, leading to increased productivity and overall satisfaction in your endeavors.

E. Cultivate gratitude:

Be thankful for what you have and for those around you who support you—be it your parents, friends, or your mentor. Take some time to go to them and tell them how much their presence means to you. Let them know the value they add to your life and how their support plays a key role in your journey.

Benefit: Cultivating gratitude helps shift your perspective towards a more positive outlook, enhances your overall well-being, and deepens your sense of contentment and fulfillment.

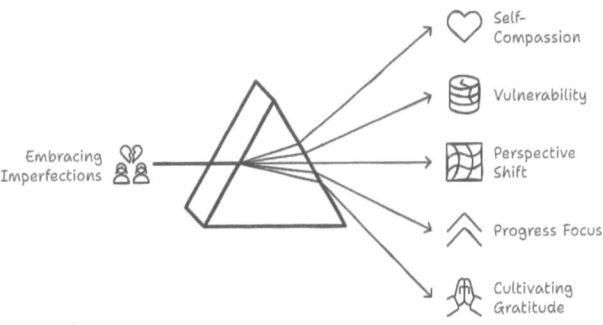

By adopting these strategies, you can pave the way for a more fulfilling and genuine existence, embracing your true self and the beauty of imperfection.

<u>Here's a to-do list after this chapter "Embracing Imperfections":</u>

1. <u>Self-Reflection:</u>

- Write down a list of your imperfections and any negative self-talk that accompanies them.
- Challenge these negative thoughts by questioning their validity and considering alternative, more compassionate perspectives.

2. <u>Practice Self-Compassion:</u>

- Whenever you catch yourself being self-critical, replace it with a positive affirmation or a compassionate statement.
- Make time for self-care activities that support your physical, emotional, and mental wellness.

3. <u>Cultivate Gratitude:</u>

- Start a gratitude journal or dedicate a few moments each day to reflect on things you appreciate about yourself and your life.
- Share your gratitude with others by expressing appreciation for their imperfections and the unique qualities they bring to the world.

4. <u>Set Realistic Expectations:</u>

- Recognize that striving for perfection is unrealistic and can lead to unnecessary stress and self-doubt.
- Establish realistic goals and expectations for yourself, considering your abilities, limitations, and the value of the process rather than just the result.

- Celebrate every step forward and cheer for the little wins! Every achievement, no matter how small, deserves a celebration!

5. <u>Seek Support:</u>

- Share your journey with trusted friends, family members, or a therapist, and discuss the challenges and triumphs you experience.
- Join a support group or community focusing on self-acceptance and personal growth, where you can learn from others' experiences and share your insights.

6. <u>Practice Acceptance:</u>

- Accept that imperfections are an inherent part of being human, and they do not diminish your worth or value as a person.
- Release the need for constant validation or approval from others and focus on self-acceptance.

Remember, embracing imperfections is a lifelong journey. Be patient with yourself and keep going.

Celebrate Your Journey

**LESSON**:- Hey Champ, Congratulations on completing the "Embracing Imperfections" chapter! You've accomplished a journey to understand self-discovery and growth, and now it's time to put your newfound knowledge into practical action. Remember, embracing imperfections is not about striving for perfection; it's about accepting and loving yourself, flaws and all.

Chapter - 8
A Game of the Senses

POV:- In a world brimming with distractions, learning to manage our minds is super important! Our thoughts can feel overwhelmed with all the information coming at us, making it tough to stay focused, productive, and at peace. In this chapter, we'll dive into some friendly, practical tips to help you regain control over your mind. Together, we can find ways to feel centered, focused, and free from those pesky distractions!

"Let's dive into the fascinating world of the senses!"

In a world filled with different experiences, our senses can simultaneously be both a wonderful gift and a significant challenge. The things we see, the sounds we hear, the foods we taste, the friends we spend time with, our sense of smell, and all other sensations that surround us have the power to both captivate and overwhelm our minds. They influence our emotions, shape our perceptions, and often impact our decisions. But what if we could harness this power and take control over our senses? What if we could navigate the world of sensations with intention and purpose? This chapter delves into the art of understanding our senses better and the positive impact it can have on our lives. Let's start our journey by realizing the power of our senses.

"Have you ever noticed how your sense of discipline seems to pack its bags and leave for a vacation when you're at work?"

There are many things in life that are indulging our senses in other ways and for that reason, we all need to understand that controlling our senses in a human form of life is very important. We can generally observe that when we plan for something, whether it is to upgrade ourselves in spiritual life, learn a new skill, or enroll in a new course, our senses start acting like it's on strike, senses are like I would not let you move forward until I get satisfied. This is normal with most humans if you've ever observed.

It's like when you're working, and a friend invites you on a short trip—you often don't say no. Or, if you're studying and your loved one calls to chat, many of us will drop our work to talk and have fun. This is a common reality for most of us because our senses aren't following our planned schedule; they're chasing immediate pleasures, which rarely involve productive tasks.

Ofcourse, going on a date with someone you really like instead working for your goal or eating quick and tasty junk food instead of cooking something healthy feels more satisfying at the moment. But we seriously need to rethink that while we're letting these things happen at the moment we let our senses take control of ourselves.

At that time, we started thinking like we'll be working after enjoying 15 minutes of a funny video or, after 30 minutes meeting a friend or, after 15 minutes talking to our girlfriend or boyfriend but when these short breaks turn into longer periods, we don't even realize.

Eventually, we feel guilty for not studying or working as our scheduled plan and feel we've wasted time unproductively.

It's like you've started doing a lecture and suddenly a thought comes into your mind provoking a scene of a web series that you liked the most and then you close the lecture and open another screen to watch that scene from that drama end up completing the whole series, or it's like you're working on something and your phone beeps and when you see the notification, it's the message from a person whom you have a crush upon and then what happens generally is

I think I don't need to give an explanation about because you all better understand the scenario.

This is what distracts our focus from a productive to a distracted phase of our lives and once we diverted from the main task that we've planned to do, we lost somewhere in getting the pleasure to satisfy the desire of our senses. And this is not a newly founded problem among most people.

There are various humans we see and meet in our daily lives and everyone is different from one another, either in the way of how they think, how they cultivate a situation, or how they take their level of intelligence to understand different perspectives, and many more things. There are various qualitative differences you can find between you and other person and that's okay because no one can be the same, so when we compare ourselves with someone else's abilities, someone else's interest, and their competence, we end up getting only disappointment and a lack of satisfaction in ourself.

In your home also sometimes might your parents have compared you with someone else and said *"Wo dekho sharma ji ka ladka kitni achi job kar raha hai, aur ek tum!"* and if you haven't faced this scenario at your home then you must be the lucky one. Actually, they're not wrong, our loved ones just want to see us being successful, but in some way that others became in their perspective.

As everyone is different with their perspective of growth, their problems, their sight of distractions, and their focus would also bring the same difference. So first of all, we should understand to never get overwhelmed by comparing ourselves with any other person whom we think they are better, neither you should feel down by seeing or interacting with someone with something better than you. It's because, in today's time, we compare a lot which results in depriving our mindsets. We, people, should not suppress our desires, rather we should search for something else that can help us move out from that problem of losing control over our senses.

Once upon a time, in a lively city filled with bright lights and noise, there lived a young woman named Maya. A passionate writer, she loved life but often felt overwhelmed by the city's distractions.

One day, Maya decided to take a break and went to a peaceful mountain retreat where her grandmother lived. As soon as she arrived, the fresh air and soothing sounds of nature wrapped around her, bringing a sense of calm she hadn't felt since a longer duration.

While being there, she attended a mindfulness workshop led by a wise teacher. Everyone was sharing their experiences at that workshop. Looking at everyone else she also shared her struggles with focus, and then the mentor at that workshop offered this insightful lesson:

"Think of your mind as a lake. When the surface is calm, you can see all the way to the bottom, noticing everything beneath. But when the waters get stirred up, everything becomes cloudy and unclear. Life will always try to stir your waters, but with practice, you can learn to calm them down, allowing you to see clearly, even in the midst of chaos."

Maya reflected on this and began practicing mindfulness, allowing her thoughts to flow without getting caught up in them. Day by day, she felt lighter and more focused.

When she returned to the city, Maya transformed her home into a sanctuary of peace, minimized distractions, and embraced healthy habits. She remembered the lesson of the lake and stayed calm when challenges arose.

Over time, Maya found a beautiful balance between city life and inner peace. She joyfully shared her story with others, inspiring them to find their own calm amid the chaos, reminding everyone that true clarity comes from within.

TAKE THE CONTROL OF YOUR SENSES - "THE RUBIK'S CUBE METHOD"

We all want to be disciplined and less distracted in our lives and we also follow many things even if you ever search on the internet, how to control your mind, and your senses, the internet would also provide you with hundreds or thousands of tactics, but I would be glad to share a different approach that I personally follow to get control over the senses and being disciplined in all way possible.

In today's fast-paced world, distractions are everywhere, constantly hindering our ability to focus on important tasks. Whether it's studying, working, or pursuing personal goals, staying focused and avoiding distractions has become a significant challenge. However, by employing a unique and practical approach, we can utilize the Rubik's Cube method to not only distract ourselves from temptations but also enhance our productivity.

The Rubik's Cube as a Symbol of Distraction:

The Rubik's Cube, a 3D combination puzzle, serves as an ideal symbol for the distractions that often lure us away from our intended tasks. Just as the colorful cube tempts us with the urge to solve it, various thoughts, desires, and external stimuli frequently divert our attention from what truly matters at hand. By consciously embracing this diversion and transforming it into a tool for self-improvement, we can reframe distractions as opportunities for growth and enhanced productivity.

The Rubik's Cube Challenge:

Imagine this: you're getting ready to study or work, but just as you start, your mind begins to wander, pulling you toward all sorts of distractions. To help keep your focus, you grab a colorful Rubik's Cube and place it nearby, its bright colors catching your eye.

Whenever you feel the urge to lose focus, you challenge yourself to solve the cube. You set a timer for five minutes and start twisting and turning the cube, trying to line up all the colors on each side.

If you manage to solve it before the timer goes off, you get to enjoy a guilt-free 30-minute break to do something you love. But if time runs out and you haven't finished, it's a reminder to get back to your work. This fun approach turns solving a puzzle into a helpful tool to boost your concentration and self-discipline, making your study time both productive and enjoyable..

Transforming Distraction into Motivation:

As you begin to tackle the Rubik's Cube, the distractions that initially tempted you will lose their power. By setting a time limit and actively engaging your mind in a puzzle-solving activity, you redirect your focus away from unproductive thoughts and desires. The Rubik's Cube acts as a physical manifestation of the distraction, allowing you to confront it head-on while maintaining a connection to your original goal.

Triggering Self-Realization and Returning to Productivity:

During the Rubik's Cube challenge, the noise of distractions fades into the background. As you strive to align the colors within the time limit, your mind becomes triggered by a sense of urgency and self-realization. You become acutely aware that you are potentially wasting your productive time on silly unnecessary matters. This realization prompts you to refocus your energy and prioritize the task you initially set out to accomplish.

It's Benefits and Practicality:

The Rubik's Cube method offers several benefits and practical applications:

1. <u>Enhanced Productivity</u>: By using the Rubik's Cube as a diversionary tactic, you transform distractions into a

catalyst for productivity, ultimately accomplishing your intended tasks.

2. <u>Improved Focus and Concentration</u>: The method sharpens your ability to concentrate, trains your mind to ignore unnecessary distractions, and maintain focus on important objectives.

3. <u>Breaking the Cycle of Bad Habits</u>: Over time, this method helps eliminate harmful patterns and promotes better self-discipline.

4. <u>Engaging the Senses</u>: It's a very hands-on experience that engages your senses, boosts your brain activity, and helps improve your mental sharpness.

<u>Conclusion:</u>

In a world overflowing with distractions, The Rubik's Cube method serves as a powerful tool in our quest for greater efficiency and self-improvement, enabling us to overcome distractions and achieve our goals.

*<u>**To-Do List for Harnessing Sensory Discipline and Enhancing Productivity:**</u>*

<u>1. Identify Sensory Distractions:</u> Take a moment to reflect on the sensory distractions that affect your focus and productivity. Consider what pulls your attention away—whether it's social media notifications, loud noises, or visual clutter.

<u>2. Create a Sensory-Friendly Workspace:</u> Designate a specific area as your work zone to foster calmness and concentration. Clear away unnecessary clutter, keep distracting digital devices at bay, organize your belongings neatly, and incorporate elements like plants or calming scents to cultivate a serene environment.

<u>3. Engage in Mindfulness Exercises:</u> Set aside a few minutes each day for mindfulness activities that enhance your sensory awareness. This could be deep breathing,

meditation, or simply observing your surroundings with greater attention.

4. Limit Digital Distractions: If keeping your digital devices away is challenging, establish boundaries for your screen time. Explore apps that help manage duration and silence notifications during focused work sessions. Allocate specific times for checking emails or social media.

5. Adopt a Minimalist Approach: Simplify both your physical and digital environments. Declutter your workspace and organize your digital files to reduce visual and mental distractions, allowing for a clearer focus.

6. Incorporate Exercise into Your Routine: Choose physical activities you love—be it yoga, running, dancing, or any other form of exercise that invigorates you. This will boost both your energy levels and productivity.

7. Utilize the Rubik's Cube Method: When distractions arise, consider using the Rubik's Cube as a fun diversion. Challenge yourself to solve it within a set time, using this task as a tool for self-reflection and a way to refocus your attention.

8. Practice Self-Compassion and Persistence: Remember that enhancing your productivity and managing distractions is a journey. Be kind to yourself when setbacks occur, and nurture a resilient mindset.

By incorporating these strategies into your daily routine, you can foster sensory discipline, gain control over your focus, and significantly boost your productivity.

The following illustrates the key considerations we must keep in mind following the conclusion of this chapter:

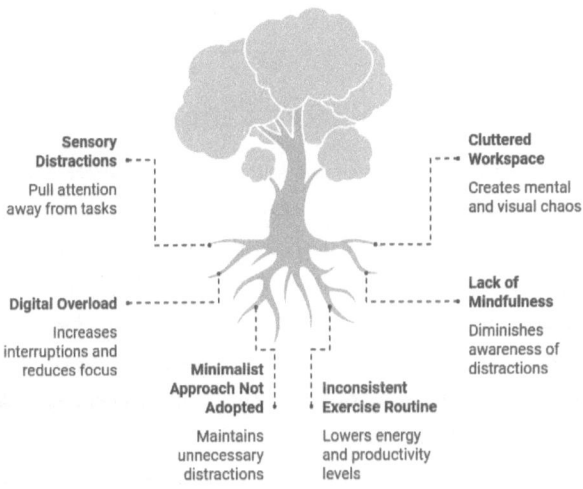

Enhancing Focus and Productivity

- **Sensory Distractions** — Pull attention away from tasks
- **Cluttered Workspace** — Creates mental and visual chaos
- **Digital Overload** — Increases interruptions and reduces focus
- **Lack of Mindfulness** — Diminishes awareness of distractions
- **Minimalist Approach Not Adopted** — Maintains unnecessary distractions
- **Inconsistent Exercise Routine** — Lowers energy and productivity levels

LESSON:- Congratulations you've completed the chapter that shows your willingness to learn more. Always remember that by embracing sensory discipline and employing practical techniques like the Rubik's Cube method, we can transform distractions into opportunities for growth.

Chapter - 9
A Change for Goodness

POV:- *In today's world, everyone has their unique perspective, which is pretty amazing! But it's important to understand the difference between just doing good things and truly nurturing goodness in our lives. "A Change for Goodness" presents a compelling perspective that advocates for personal transformation as the cornerstone of creating a better world. Let's take some time to reflect on what we consider to be good or bad. By doing this, we can discover the changes that can bring more positivity into our minds and lives. Together, we can learn how to spread goodness and make our lives richer and more meaningful!*

Hey there! We all have those moments when life feels a bit overwhelming, right? But the awesome thing is that we each carry a little spark of hope inside us. That tiny flicker can grow into a bright flame of change, lighting up the world around us!

So, how do we start this exciting journey toward a brighter future? It all begins with taking that first step, changing our mindset, and welcoming personal growth. Let's team up and see how we can all be a positive force together! By diving into empathy, resilience, and the magic of teamwork, we can truly make a difference. Let's do this!

Let's open our hearts and minds and set off on this exciting path of transformation, sparking the light of change for a better tomorrow!

In this big world, each person has something good and bad within them. Being good brings a positive mindset and happiness in many ways. However, we all have some negative traits too, like being rude, having a big ego, or being selfish. It's important to remember that nobody can be perfect or flawless, and we shouldn't aim for 100% perfection. But we can still strive for personal growth by learning from our mistakes and everyday experiences. Changing for the better isn't just an option; it's necessary for finding peace and happiness in life.

While we can't change other people or force them to be good, we can focus on improving ourselves. It's crucial to let go of harmful habits and behaviors that can harm important things or hurt those people we care about. But neglecting our relationships, careers, or other important aspects of life can lead to negative consequences. Unfortunately, many people only realize the extent of their mistakes when something bad happens, leaving them with regret. For example, if we let our ego or bad behavior ruin our relationships, it can lead to arguments and sometimes even breakups.

In terms of love or relationship, some people say that true love accepts a person as they are, flaws and all. But sometimes, those flaws can be destructive, like aggression, dominance, or other harmful tendencies that can damage love and connection. In those cases, it becomes crucial to change ourselves, grow, and mature to bring positive development and happiness to our lives.

If we have destructive habits or a negative mindset that can harm others or important parts of our lives, it's essential to transform ourselves. Letting go of aggression and embracing kindness and love is one of the most significant improvements we can make for ourselves.

Have you ever thought about why so many people struggle to reach their future goals? Have you tried to figure out why most people tend to give up on their dreams midway? You probably know or will meet some people like this in your life, and you might even notice a few in your own circle. It's interesting to see how common this can be!

We're going to tackle a practical approach to a generous issue that nearly everyone faces today: the tendency to lose sight of long-term goals while getting sidetracked by immediate gratification. Let's dive in and address this challenge head-on!

In today's world where people rush towards each other, it feels like everyone is chasing after fame, fortune, and a life filled with luxury. Many of us dream about driving stylish cars, living in beautiful homes, and taking amazing trips around the globe. But even with these dreams being so common, why do so many people struggle to turn them into reality?

A big part of the answer is that we often prioritize short-term pleasures over our long-term goals. Let's understand why having a long-term mindset is essential, and I'll share an interesting story to show just how powerful that approach can be!

The Trap of Instant Gratification:

Human nature is wired to seek instant gratification. We often prioritize short-term pleasures over long-term goals that require sustained effort and dedication. This mindset leads to a cycle of temporary happiness followed by long-term dissatisfaction. Many individuals lose sight of their true aspirations, overlooking the bigger picture in pursuit of immediate happiness. Let me share a story that makes you understand the point that we are targeting here.

The Story of Raju: A bright student until he experienced the pleasure of instant gratification.

Let's consider the story of Raju, a bright student who was determined to top his 12th-grade board exams. Six months before the exams, Raju confidently declared his ambition to his friends, saying he would achieve academic excellence. However, just one month before the exams, Raju met someone special and found himself completely engrossed in a new relationship. He started neglecting his studies, losing focus on his long-term goals and all. It is not like we people should not have fun, not make new friends and all. It just should be in a manner and control that does not become the reason for destruction and diversion from our long-term happiness and vision.

Raju's story is not unique. Many individuals, even you get sometimes swayed by immediate pleasures and forget your long-term objectives. Nowadays We become consumed by short-term happiness, oblivious to the fact that it distracts us from its ultimate source of fulfillment. And if anyone is facing the same, they need to understand the importance of balancing between both, short-term pleasure and long-term goals.

The Importance of Balancing Immediate Gratification and Long-Term Goals:

While it's natural to seek joy in the present, it is crucial to strike a balance between immediate gratification and long-term aspirations. Here are some ways that I personally used to achieve that balance:

1. Set Clear Goals: Define your long-term goals clearly and outline the steps needed to accomplish them. Establishing a roadmap will keep you focused and motivated.

2. Embrace Self-Discipline: Boost your self-discipline to block distractions and stay focused on your long-term goals. Build strong habits that lead you toward your aspirations while resisting short-term temptations.

3. Delayed Gratification: Follow the concept of delayed gratification. Understand that postponing instant pleasures in favor of long-term rewards can lead to greater fulfillment and success.

4. Seek Support and Accountability: Surround yourself with individuals who encourage and support your long-

term objectives. Join communities or find mentors who can provide guidance and hold you accountable.

Conclusion:

To achieve true success and fulfillment, it is important to resist immediate gratification and focus on long-term goals. While short-term pleasures can provide temporary happiness, they often lead to regret and hinder greater progress. By adopting a long-term approach, individuals can maintain focus, persevere through challenges, and ultimately reach their desired outcomes, leading to genuine happiness and accomplishment.

Explore these actionable to-do lists inspired by insights from "A Change for Goodness" to turn your intentions into actions!

1. Reflect on Your Long-Term Goals: Take time to reflect on your long-term aspirations and write them down. Define what success and happiness mean to you personally.

2. Identify Immediate Gratification Traps: Be aware of the short-term pleasures that may hinder your progress toward your long-term goals. Recognize habits that contribute to instant gratification and make a conscious effort to avoid or minimize them.

3. Create a Roadmap: Break down your long-term goals into smaller, achievable tasks upon which you can actively work.

4. Practice Self-Discipline: Cultivate self-discipline by developing daily habits and routines that align with your long-term goals.

5. Embrace Delayed Gratification: Train yourself to delay immediate gratification in favor of long-term rewards.

6. Seek Accountability: Share your long-term goals with a trusted friend, mentor, or family member. Ask them to hold you accountable and provide support and guidance

along the way. Regular check-ins and discussing progress to keep you pumped and on the same target on what you want.

7. <u>Surround Yourself with Like-Minded Individuals:</u> Seek out individuals who share similar long-term goals or are on a similar journey of personal growth. Join communities, attend workshops or events, or connect with like-minded individuals online. .

Personal growth takes time and effort. Be patient, celebrate small victories, and stay committed to your long-term vision. By taking practical steps, you can improve yourself and contribute to a better world.

Here is a visual that reflects the crux of this chapter:

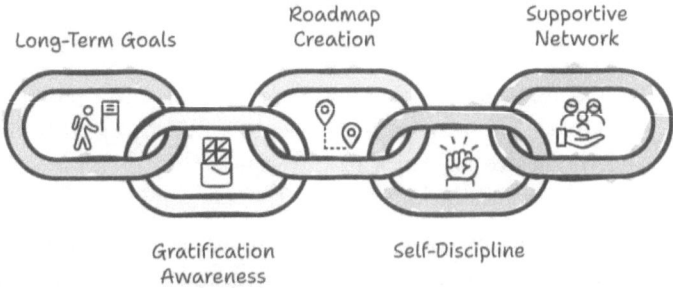

LESSON:- Embrace change for lasting happiness. Focus on personal growth, set clear goals, and prioritize long-term gains over instant gratification to achieve a brighter future.

Chapter - 10
The outcome of patience

POV:- *My friend! I'm glad you're here! Today, we'll discuss something exciting that can bring one more qualitative aspect to our lives: patience. In our busy world, it's tempting to rush through everything. We want to progress in our jobs, start amazing businesses, build great portfolios, strengthen our relationships, and many more—often all at once! But is this the best approach?*

What do you think is better: taking your time or trying to do it all at once? Let's explore why patience matters.

As we explored in the previous chapter, "A Change for Goodness," we learned how the lure of instant gratification and the desire for quick results can lead us down a path of distraction and darkness.

In this chapter, we will delve into how, in our fast-paced world, patience is often overlooked and undervalued. We live in a society where we made things like waiting as a burden, where impatience holds sway.

Imagine this: you're at home, feeling hungry as time passes, and you can smell your favorite food from Zomato in your mind. You placed your order, but it seems to take forever to arrive. As the minutes go by, you start to feel frustrated. It's easy to think about yelling at the delivery person or blaming the restaurant for the delay.

Now, picture this: after you calm down, you get a notification explaining the hold-up. Your heart sank when you found out that the delivery person was on their way but had to rush home because their wife suddenly collapsed. At that moment, you realize how quickly we were to judge and show anger without knowing what was really happening.

Thinking about this, you might feel regret. It reminds us that it's important to be patient and understanding. Our reactions can affect our mental well-being. Instead of reacting right away, taking a moment to consider the other person's situation could lead to a better outcome for both sides.

Patience, at its core, is a virtue that allows us to weather the storms of life with grace and resilience. It is the art of remaining calm and composed in the face of challenges, delays, and setbacks. While it may seem elusive in a world that constantly demands our immediate attention, patience holds the key to unlocking a host of benefits that can transform our lives.

Do you ever feel that patience can heal or repair something? Yes, you heard it right, it can help repair broken things like relationships and businesses and sometimes guide us in making better choices, improve our mental health, and help us reach our long-term goals. If you often feel restless during tough times, crave quick results, or feel overwhelmed by life's challenges, join us here. Together, we will reveal the positive changes that come to those who choose to develop themselves.

To truly understand the outcomes of patience, it is essential to establish a clear definition and delve into its delicate aspects. Patience can be defined as the ability to maintain composure and stay calm in the face of adversity, delays, or challenges. It is the art of embracing a state of mind that resists the impulses of frustration, allowing for a more measured and thoughtful approach to life's trials.

It is not merely the act of waiting for something to happen; it is a mindset that enables us to navigate through life's obstacles with a calmness of resilience and grace. It is about accepting that certain things are beyond our immediate control and having the wisdom to recognize that, time, effort, and perseverance are often required for favorable outcomes.

The outcome is complex. In relationships, patience helps create understanding, empathy, and good communication. By controlling our impulses and taking the time to listen and understand, we can form stronger connections, resolve conflicts peacefully, and build healthier relationships with our loved ones.

Have you ever found yourself at a crossroads, grappling with an important decision that leaves you feeling a bit confused?

Have you ever found yourself in a tricky situation where you had to make a big decision, and timing played a crucial role? Let's say you're thinking about buying a new iPad and signing up for an MBA course, with a budget of 1 lakh for both. After doing a bit of research, you see that the regular iPad is priced at 40,000. But hold on! There's a better model with cool features available for just an extra 20,000.

Now, the MBA course costs 60,000, and you're working with a total budget of 100,000. Just as you start weighing your options, you get a call from an executive at another institution. They have a fantastic offer: if you enroll within the next 12 hours, you'll snag a whopping 40% discount on the MBA course!

What's the first thought that pops into your head? Chances are, you'll lose your patience and be eager to grab that amazing discount and save some extra cash for the upgraded iPad. It sounds great and could make you really happy right now! But here's the catch—if you rush into choosing the discounted classes and they don't meet your expectations, will it truly be worth the savings? It's definitely something to think about!

It's similar to going to a mall and being drawn in by various appealing offers; if an offer catches your eye, you might spend your hard-earned money on it without considering whether it's something you truly need.

It comes in many forms. It often manifests when something is delayed, when situations turn unfavorable, or during disagreements with family or friends when our perspectives clash.

In those moments, expressing our thoughts might bring short-term satisfaction, but what about the long-term effects? How do we truly feel after such conflicts? Have you ever taken a moment to reflect on it?

Everything in life requires patience, whether you're starting a new business, embarking on a new career, launching a YouTube channel, or entering a new relationship. Without patience, it becomes difficult for things to progress positively.

By embracing its power, we open doors to personal growth, harmonious relationships, improved decision-making, emotional well-being, and enhanced problem-solving skills.

Benefits and positive outcomes of practicing patience:

1. IMPROVED RELATIONSHIPS: Patience fosters better communication, empathy, and understanding in relationships.

2. ENHANCED DECISION-MAKING: Patience enables us to make wiser and more thoughtful decisions. By taking the time to consider all options and potential outcomes, we can avoid hasty choices and make decisions aligned with our values and long-term goals.

3. EMOTIONAL WELL-BEING: Patience contributes to emotional resilience and reduces stress levels. It helps us maintain a positive mindset, preventing unnecessary frustration and promoting inner peace.

4. IMPROVED PROBLEM-SOLVING: It allows for a calm and clear mindset when facing problems.

5. <u>**ENHANCED EMPATHY AND UNDERSTANDING**</u>: Patience opens our hearts to empathize with others and understand their perspectives.

Remember, "Practicing patience helps you find peace and joy within." When you choose not to get angry or yell at others when you feel frustrated, you protect your mental health and keep your inner peace. If your mind turns negative, it's like carrying a ticking bomb inside, ready to disrupt your calm.

These are just some of the benefits and positive outcomes that can result from practicing patience.

<u>Here are some actionable steps for your to-do list to develop patience and practice it for better outcomes:</u>

1. <u>Identify Triggers:</u> Reflect on the situations or circumstances that often test your patience. Be aware of your triggers, such as traffic jams, long lines, or challenging conversations. Recognizing these triggers will help you prepare and respond with patience.

2. <u>Pause and Breathe</u>: When faced with a patience-testing situation, pause for a moment and take a deep breath. Breathing exercises can help calm your mind, regulate your emotions, and provide a buffer between the trigger and your response.

3. <u>Practice Active Listening:</u> Focus on actively listening to others without interrupting or rushing to respond. Give them your full attention and strive to understand their perspective before offering your own. Practice patience in conversations by allowing space for others to express themselves fully.

4. <u>Embrace Delays:</u> Embrace delays and unexpected changes as opportunities to practice patience. Instead of becoming frustrated, use these moments to practice acceptance and find alternative ways to make the most of the situation.

5. <u>Practice Empathy Daily:</u> Incorporate acts of empathy into your daily routine. Whether it's lending a listening ear to a friend or offering a helping hand to someone in need, acts of empathy cultivate patience and understanding toward others.

6. <u>Reflect and Learn:</u> Identify what triggered your impatience and how you could have responded differently. Use these reflections as learning opportunities to grow and improve your patience.

7. <u>Celebrate Progress:</u> When you find yourself responding with patience in situations that previously tested you, give yourself credit and celebrate the positive outcomes that arise from your patient approach.

Incorporating small actionable steps into your daily routine can help you build patience, leading to better outcomes in life. With patience, you can strengthen relationships, improve decision-making, and enhance emotional well-being. It helps you tackle challenges with resilience and makes your journey through life even more rewarding!

LESSON:- To our readers, Embrace the power of patience in your life, and you will witness the remarkable outcomes it can bring. May your journey be filled with resilience, understanding, and the rewards that come from embracing patience along the way.

Chapter - 11
Emotional intelligence

POV:- In this chapter, I'm excited to initiate into the amazing power of emotional intelligence! In a world where connections and relationships matter so much, emotional intelligence stands out as a game-changer. We'll explore how being self-aware, empathetic, and a great communicator can lead to personal growth, professional success, and truly meaningful interactions. Get ready for a journey that will help you understand and embrace the power of your emotions!

Hey there! I'd love to hear your thoughts on the term "Emotional Intelligence." Do you think of it as just understanding emotions, or is it something bigger, something more meaningful?

For me, emotional intelligence means so much more. When you dig a little deeper, you can see how it really helps us grow as individuals and guides us on the journey to discovering our inner wisdom. What do you think?

You know, we often hear about two main types of quotients that we all have: the first is "IQ," or Intelligence Quotient, and the second is "EQ," which stands for Emotional Quotient. Most of us have probably heard someone say, "Wow, you have a really high IQ!" And that makes sense, right? IQ is what often gets recognized when we talk about being smart or quick-thinking.

But have you ever stopped to think about your EQ? How well do you understand your own emotions, or the feelings swirling around you? Let's take a moment to reflect on that—it's just as essential as IQ, and it plays a big role in how we connect with ourselves and others!

There are times when we find ourselves approaching situations differently, and the people around us might say that we just don't understand each other. It's a common experience in our everyday lives! Sometimes, it can feel like you're not understanding someone's emotions, and at other times, they might feel the same way about you. This can lead to misunderstandings and, unfortunately, start affecting our relationships. But recognizing this can be the first step towards better communication and stronger connections!

We all know that machines are taking over many tasks as we embrace the digital age. Technology definitely makes life easier and simpler. However, there's a challenge we're facing: we sometimes start treating people like machines and become less accepting of mistakes in our workplaces, relationships, and projects. Let's remember that we're all human, and it's okay to make mistakes! Nowadays, it seems like we rely more on machines than on one another. If we take a moment to notice, we might find that while we're connecting with technology, we're unintentionally drifting away from each other.

It is important to understand that machines cannot think or feel like humans. People experience emotions, such as happiness, sadness, anger, or feeling pleasurable. These feelings influence our interactions every day.

In the future, Emotional Intelligence (EQ) will become more important. It helps us understand our emotions and those of others too. This skill will be vital in personal as well as in professional relationships. As we move forward, we will learn new ways to connect and support each other.

In workplaces, companies also value EQ as much as IQ. Employers observe that emotional skills are necessary for solving problems and working well with others. This means they will look for employees who are both smart and emotionally aware.

As we focus on our EQ, we can improve how we relate to each other. By doing this, we will create a kinder and more supportive environment for everyone. It's an important time to pay attention to our feelings and connections!

If we try to observe it thoroughly, we'll find that our both personal and professional lives are interconnected, and these both mostly depend upon our Emotional Intelligence.

Let me share a little story about my good friend Raghav. He's 29 and the main bread earner for his family. Raghav has always been super talented at what he does and tends to rise to the top in every role he takes on. Initially, he worked for a large multinational food company, but eventually, he decided to follow his dream and start his own venture.

With his previous experience, he managed to establish a startup and brought on board four more team members. Things took off really well for him, and within just three months, his company raked in an impressive 34 lakhs! However, things took a turn when a small mistake by his manager led to losing out on a significant contract. Raghav was understandably frustrated and ended up firing the manager on the spot.

After that, he became overly confident, thinking he could handle everything by himself without hiring anyone new. He put in a lot of effort, trying to manage the entire workload all alone. But as the demands of the business grew, he found it challenging to keep up. His fears about hiring someone new—worried that it might lead to losses—began to weigh heavily on him. Unfortunately, this stress spilled over into his home life, and he found himself snapping at his wife, kids, and even his parents, which left him feeling even worse afterward.

Now, let's pause for a moment and think about Raghav's situation. He acted impulsively by firing his manager without really considering all the options. Instead of addressing the underlying reasons for the contract loss, he could have focused on correcting the mistake and ensuring it didn't happen again. If he had done that, his business might be thriving even more now. Plus, if work were going well, he likely wouldn't have experienced such stress or taken it out on his family.

Another important lesson here is about being aware of his emotions. Raghav could have benefited from recognizing his feelings and managing them better. Shouting at his loved ones was not a healthy way to relieve stress. By developing his emotional intelligence, he could have equipped himself to handle unexpected challenges more effectively. This is why I believe that "Emotional Intelligence" plays a crucial role in our overall development and helps us nurture our inner wisdom.

Now, we need to be familiar with the ways that help improve our Emotional Intelligence, and we must focus on several important aspects here:

A. Take a moment to think about your emotions! It's really important to understand how we feel and reacts when a situation gets worse.

B. Understanding others' perspectives is essential, especially during challenging times. When individuals find themselves in tough situations, it can be difficult for them to navigate effectively. In these moments, seeking guidance from trusted friends or mentors who are not experiencing the same challenges can be beneficial. It's valuable to ask them for their insights on how they would approach similar circumstances. Following their advice can be advantageous, as a calm and healthy mindset often leads to more effective decision-making than one clouded by stress.

C. The next thing is that we have to pay attention to how people respond to what we say! It's really helpful to notice their facial expressions and reactions, as this helps us connect with them better. A lot of times, we get caught up in our own thoughts and feelings, leaving little room to see how others are taking our words. By observing others first, we can respond in a way that makes our conversations more meaningful.

D. Take a two-minute pause, take a deep breath, and reflect before reacting to any situation. I know this can be challenging, but often we make hasty decisions and respond impulsively, which can lead to a feeling of guilt later on.

E. Empathy – When someone makes a mistake or fails to meet our expectations, our first instinct is often to point fingers and blame them. Instead, we should take a moment to put ourselves in their shoes and consider the reasons behind their actions. By exploring their "why," we can gain a deeper understanding of their perspective and the circumstances that led to the situation.

F. Let's take a moment to consider criticism! When someone shares their thoughts or concerns about us, even if it's tough to hear, it's a great opportunity for growth. Instead of jumping to defend ourselves, why not listen to their perspective? If you find that there's some truth in what they're saying, it's a chance to think about how you can improve. And if you disagree, that's okay too—sometimes it's best to just let it go! Remember, there will always be people with varying opinions, and if we react to every little thing, we could end up feeling overwhelmed. So, let's approach these moments with an open heart and a friendly mindset! We've got this!

I hope you understand the importance of balancing our emotional intelligence and being more in tune with our emotional well-being.

We all come across plenty of information about why we should do things, thanks to the many books and people we learn from. However, there aren't as many who share the practical steps to actually make it happen in our actions. It's great to understand the reasons behind our actions, but it can be confusing when it's time to put those ideas into practice. That's why, at the end of each chapter, I'm sharing some friendly and actionable steps you can add to your to-do list.

<u>Here, This to-do list will help you develop and practice "Emotional Intelligence" in a way that can really a better emotional understanding developing a little more EQ in your life. Let's grow together!</u>

1. <u>Listen attentively:</u> Pay close attention to others when they speak, showing genuine interest and focus. Maintain eye contact and use non-verbal cues to show you're fully present in the conversation.

2. <u>Know yourself:</u> Take time for self-reflection to understand your own emotions, triggers, and how they impact your interactions with others.

3. <u>Understand others:</u> Put yourself in their shoes, seeking to grasp their feelings, needs, and experiences. Offer support, validation, and understanding during challenging times.

4. <u>Manage emotions:</u> Learn to control and regulate your emotions in different situations—practice techniques like deep breathing or taking short breaks to stay calm during stressful moments.

5. <u>Communicate effectively:</u> Express your emotions and thoughts clearly and respectfully.

By incorporating these practical applications into your life, you can actively cultivate and enhance your emotional intelligence, leading to a more harmonious and fulfilling personal and professional journey.

Pathways to Emotional Intelligence

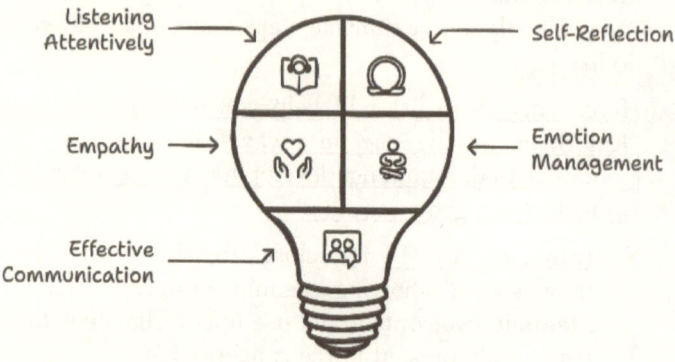

**LESSON**:-*Emotional intelligence is your guide to personal growth! By improving self-awareness and empathy, you can connect with others and tackle challenges confidently. Effective communication builds strong relationships and unlocks your potential. Embrace this journey and enjoy a fulfilling life ahead!*

Chapter - 12
The power of empathy

POV:- Get ready to dive into the captivating world of empathy, where understanding others becomes a superpower! In this chapter, we'll explore how empathy opens doors to heartfelt connections and bridges gaps in relationships.

Have you ever found yourself overwhelmed with emotions and not feeling good? When people meet you during those times, what do they usually say? Phrases like "Sab thik ho jayega" (Everything will be fine) or "Life mein ye sab hota rehta hai" (Such things happen in life) often come up. Yes, most people's responses tend to revolve around these lines. How do you feel when you hear such comments? Don't you sometimes think, "It's easy for them to say that"? It's because those giving advice may not be experiencing the same situation as you.

Hearing these common phrases can lead to increased frustration at that moment. To truly understand these overwhelming emotions, we first need to learn about empathy. So, let's discover the magic of walking in someone else's shoes, and learn how to tune into emotions.

Hey friends! Have you ever had a conversation that left you feeling really understood? You know, those moments when someone seems to truly get what you're feeling, offering comfort without needing to say a word? That's very rare and Ofcourse that's the wonderful magic of empathy!

In this chapter, we will take a friendly journey together to explore the beautiful world of empathy. A powerful quality that helps us build meaningful connections and understanding in our personal and professional relationships. We'll break down what empathy really means, and why it's so important, share some fun, and at last some practical tips on how to nurture this amazing trait in ourselves. Let's dive in!

You all must have heard about "Sympathy", which simply means the act of acknowledging and feeling sorry for someone's pain, hardship, or misfortune. It involves expressing compassion and showing concern for another person's situation. Sympathy is based on understanding someone's emotions from an outsider's perspective without necessarily experiencing those emotions yourself.

There is a big difference between Sympathy and Empathy.

Empathy goes beyond sympathy as it involves deeply understanding and sharing the feelings and perspectives of another person. It is the ability to put yourself in someone else's shoes, to experience their emotions, and to see the world from their view. Empathy requires an emotional connection and a genuine attempt to comprehend and relate to someone else's experiences, whether positive or negative.

When we respond with empathy, it creates a warm and welcoming space for others to share their feelings. They can open up to us without worrying about being judged, and that can really make a difference!

When we see someone with a problem, then we generally show some sympathy with our concerns, and the next step of that sympathy is empathy. It's about the feelings, the pain, or anything that a person is going through, when we try to feel the same, then it can be called empathy. Keeping yourself in place of others, trying to see and observe, the people, and the world, really brings a great change in our lives.

If we try to observe different people by imagining ourselves in their situations, we might stop complaining about them, about our lives. And if we follow this, we might stop searching for the negativities, the incompleteness in people around us. This is a fact that if we start following empathy and then look at people's activities, their decisions, and their actions, it might start making us feel that what they are doing, the decision they have taken, might be right somewhere in their point of view. And if we started taking things this way we would stop complaining about what they've done that makes us unfavorable or feel like a mistake, instead, we would start looking at the reasons why they've done this, and what would have been the reason behind that. And when we try to understand the situation, then we'll be able to keep ourselves in their places, and at that time we have to think what would I do if I had to make the decisions in that scenario? When we take the situations on us, we might find that, we may take things very negatively when it comes to others, but the reason that you will find through empathy, leaves a great impact on your mindset, at that time you will definitely accept that the reason was so genuine, and you'll feel completely understood of that person. In most cases, we will find that, if we were in place of others, we would have done the same as them, and that brings the situation in front when we stop looking at others negatively and uplift our understanding power which also makes our bond stronger with everyone. And this is what we can call "Empathy".

Imagine a scenario where someone's words, decisions, or unexpected actions offend us. Our immediate response might be to take it personally, feeling hurt or angry. But what if, instead of reacting impulsively, we take a moment to step into the other person's shoes? What if we tried to understand their perspective, their struggles, and the reason behind their actions? This is where the magic of empathy unfolds.

It allows us to keep ourselves in the place of others, to truly feel what they feel, to understand their pain and problems, and to grasp their motivations. It requires us to set aside our own judgments and assumptions and open our hearts and minds to the experiences of those around us. You know what we generally do, we always judge people based on our own understanding and assumptions which always fill our minds with wrong perceptions and negativities about them. This is the most feasible category we've to work on.

To truly embrace the magic of empathy, the first step is to listen with an open heart. Think about the times you've witnessed someone sharing their feelings, and someone jump in with advice or judgments before he even finished. It can be really frustrating, right?

Imagine the life of a student who's putting in all their effort but still struggling with exams. He might start to feel down, like he's not good enough, and just want to shut himself away from the world, and one day, a friend comes to meet him. This student has a lot of feelings bottled up inside, and he's looking for someone who can really understand what they're going through and when he sees his friend, a hope comes to his heart. But then, when he started sharing his feelings, instead of just listening, the friend interrupted and started pointing out everything the student could have done differently and started comparing his friend's situation with his own, offering advice based on what they thought.

First of all, we need to understand that when someone shares their personal experiences, they trust us to listen and understand. For example, if a friend talks about their recent breakup, they expect our support. Instead of merely listening, we might unintentionally shift the focus to our own experiences, implying that their pain is less significant than ours. This can happen when we compare their feelings to our own, instead of fully hearing them out. When we do this, it can make them feel ignored and insecure. It's important to prioritize being a good listener and providing the support they need in that moment.

How do you think that makes him feel? It's a situation we can all relate to at some point in our lives. If we truly want to embrace the magic of empathy, we need to focus on really becoming a good listener first. It's all about creating a safe space for sharing and understanding.

The benefits of embracing empathy are abundant.

Whether it's a friendship, a relationship, or any business venture, whether you're a leader somewhere, a mentor to someone, an important part of your family, or a friend of someone, if you bring Empathy into practice, it'll improve you in overall management.

In any kind of relationship—be it romantic, friendship, or something else—it's totally normal for people to see things differently. And you know what? That's completely okay! It's what makes our connections unique and interesting. It's important to recognize that we won't always see eye to eye. This is where empathy plays a crucial role. By stepping into someone else's shoes, we can better understand what they are bringing to the table, which may reflect their unique viewpoint. When we engage with our partners through empathy, we can resolve conflicts with kindness and understanding. This approach helps us find common ground and fosters a deeper sense of trust and intimacy in our relationships.

In our professional lives, empathy has a transformative impact as well. We interact with many people on a regular basis, and there are times when we feel as though they don't understand us. For example, if you are a leader in your organization and an employee under your supervision does something you find unsatisfactory, your immediate reaction may not always be the most effective response to the situation. This is where empathy comes into play. It enables us to better understand our colleagues, clients, and customers, resulting in more effective communication, collaboration, and problem-solving. By practicing empathy in the workplace, we can create a warm and inclusive culture where everyone feels respected and understood. When employees feel this way, they start working for their leader as if it were their own work, putting in a little extra effort.

So how do we enhance our capacity for empathy in practical ways?

It starts with active listening. When immersed in a conversation, embrace the art of active listening to forge a genuine connection with the other person's words and unspoken emotions. Be present, set aside distractions, and focus on understanding their words, tone, and non-verbal cues. Seek to understand their perspective by asking open-ended questions and showing genuine curiosity.

Furthermore, it requires self-awareness. Take the time to understand your own emotions, biases, and triggers. Recognize when you may be inclined to judge or become defensive. By cultivating self-awareness, you can better manage your own reactions and respond with empathy and kindness.

Ultimately, it's about making a conscious choice to prioritize understanding and compassion over judgment and anger. By making empathy more accessible and readily available in our interactions, we can create a happier, more harmonious world.

So, Let our hearts listen, seek to understand before passing judgment, and approach others with kindness and compassion. By doing so, we will not only strengthen our bonds but also contribute to a more empathetic and interconnected society.

Everyone is learning here, but we benefit from our learnings only when we apply them in our lives practically.

<u>So, here I'm giving you a to-do list to practice empathy after getting the concept from this chapter:</u>

1. <u>Practice active listening:</u> Make a conscious effort to fully listen to others without interruptions, distractions, or judgment.

2. <u>Practice perspective-taking:</u> Put yourself in someone else's shoes to understand their experiences, feelings, and motivations.

3. <u>Validate emotions:</u> Acknowledge and validate the emotions of others, letting them know that their feelings are heard and respected.

4. <u>Avoid assumptions:</u> Challenge your assumptions and refrain from making quick judgments about others without understanding their perspective.

5. <u>Practice empathy in conflict resolution:</u> When conflicts arise, approach them with empathy and a willingness to understand the other person's point of view.

6. <u>Practice empathy in leadership:</u> Incorporate empathy into your leadership style by considering the needs and perspectives of your team members.

Always remember, that developing empathy is an ongoing journey that requires consistent practice and reflection. By incorporating these to-do lists into your daily life, you can cultivate a more empathetic mindset and contribute to building stronger, more meaningful relationships.

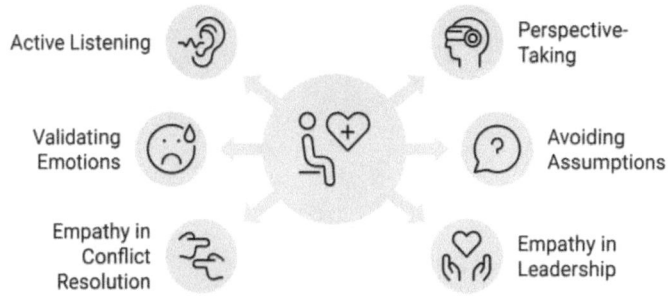

Empathy Practices

LESSON:- Make empathy a daily habit. Listen carefully and respond kindly. Be aware of your feelings, and question your beliefs. Building empathy helps create stronger connections and a more caring world.

Chapter - 13
Don't just exist, live!

POV:- In this chapter, we'll dive into the amazing benefits of living with purpose, passion, and authenticity. It's time to let go of the ordinary and welcome a life that truly feels alive! Let's explore how you can go beyond just existing and tap into the incredible potential that's already within you. Get ready to join this journey of self-discovery and embrace a life that brings you joy and fulfillment!

Have you ever felt like life is slipping away, and you're merely going through the motions? Do you find yourself caught in the trap of routine, **wishing for something a little more exciting or meaningful?**

I think everyone has sometimes felt this, right?

Have you ever taken a moment to reflect on the fascinating world of emotions? There's a certain magic that unfolds when we passionately chase our interests and watch our dreams transform into vibrant realities, bringing a smile of satisfaction to our faces.

It's a sensation that stirs the very core of our being, as our hearts are filled with a surge of pure bliss, As tranquility fills the air, when we move towards what we really want, it gracefully touches every corner of our world, our beautiful lives.

Friends, have you ever taken a moment to truly observe the moments when birds spread their wings and move on to fly, their melodious chirping echoing through the air? Or witnessed the graceful dance of water while enjoying nature by sitting beside a river, as it forms mesmerizing waves that sing harmoniously? If you experience these moments, you'll discover that they carry a great message of joy. It's like they dance and play, saying, "I am full of happiness, and you can see it in what I do!" Nature's gentle touch helps us feel better and lifts our spirits.

In the symphony of life, we often become caught up in busyness, forgetting to appreciate the magical wonders around us, that we feel, that sometimes make us smile. However, if we pause for a moment, fully present in the now, we unlock a world illuminated by the magic of emotions.

Today, while I was working on this chapter, my mom stepped into my room with some delicious cakes for me! I don't know what magic moms add to their food, but she is incredibly talented in the kitchen. She often bakes not only cakes but also amazing snacks using our everyday ingredients. Today, she sent some cake treats to a few of our relatives, and they all loved them! It warmed her heart to see their happy faces and to hear their compliments about how tasty the cake was. A bunch of them even suggested she should start a cake and snacks business to share that homey goodness with everyone. How awesome would that be?

She was excited by their ideas and looked at me with a big smile, saying, "Beta, hamein cake aur snacks ka order lena shuru karna hai," (Dear, we should start taking orders for cakes and snacks.) I have always enjoyed being adventurous and chasing my business dreams! When someone talks about things I love, like starting a business, writing, or traveling, I feel very happy. It brings me a lot of joy!

I even tried my hand at starting my first business, but unfortunately, it didn't work out as planned. Honestly, I never felt disheartened, though. It was a valuable experience, and I learned a lot from it! Afterward, I decided to take a little break to dive deeper into research and expand my knowledge for whatever comes next. I'm excited about the future!

But when she said she wanted to start a business and told me to do a bit of research and plan for her, I felt a spark of excitement! It was like someone lit a fire of happiness inside me. I truly believe that we all have a passion for something—like my love for writing and entrepreneurship—just waiting to be ignited. Like me, you also must have something that would be so powerful and inspiring! It motivates us to chase after our dreams with enthusiasm and determination. As we dive into this new adventure together, I can't wait to see the magic that happens when we follow what we really love!

There's something truly amazing about our dreams coming to life, turning from simple ideas into real, wonderful experiences. It reminds us of the incredible power we have to make our lives as beautiful as we desire to have. Every success we achieve is a testament to the magic that happens when we follow our hearts and passions.

So, my friend, let's embrace the enchantment that surrounds us. Let's wholeheartedly believe in the transformative power of emotions, and the fulfillment that comes from living in harmony with our dreams. Just as the birds sing their melodies and the waves dance in rhythmic harmony, let our lives resonate with the joyful symphony of passion, purpose, and magic that resides within us all.

I wanted to share something that's really important to me. I also wanted to raise awareness about perspectives that keep us away from moving forward. Through my writing, I felt a need to highlight issues like superstition and some pesky misguided beliefs. I also have this adventurous spirit that I just can't shake! But as life has a way of doing, I hope to get time for it soon.

For a while, my writing took a backseat as I focused on the responsibilities that life had placed before me. Though my heart yearned to continue sharing my thoughts and challenging societal norms, the demands of everyday life took precedence.

Once I had started approaching my life as a monotonous routine, moving through each day like a mechanical existence. However, a change developed when a significant incident occurred. You see, there was a time when I decided to venture to a place that had gained a reputation for being haunted—a place where people supposedly disappeared without a trace, I chose the place because I used to come there to play with my friends in my childhood but now it became superstitions in people's mind there, it's like a scary mind has filled their thoughts. Yet, I was never one to believe in such tales. I was always eager to embrace thrilling experiences that stirred my innermost being.

So, I decided to explore this place again. It was said to harbor the oldest Villa, standing for centuries, weathered by time. I packed my bags, hopped into my car, and moved on this journey. After some time, I arrived at the location, and as I stepped out, a glimmer of light caught my eye, reflecting through the window of the Villa.

I felt a bit scared, but my curiosity was stronger. I quietly walked to the window to look inside, and what I saw left me shocked. Inside the old villa, there was a woman with two children. It was clear in my mind that they had sought refuge within the confines of this ancient Villa. Without hesitation, I entered, and as they heard my footsteps, they, as usual, tried to evoke fear within me. Yet, I remained unaffected, for I had already glimpsed their true nature.

Assuring them that I meant no harm, I requested that they reveal their true faces before me. Firstly, they didn't respond but after my request, they got the comfort of believing, and then One by one, the children timidly stepped forward. One child, in particular, caught my attention. He appeared as though he hadn't bathed in ages. I attempted to engage him in conversation, but initially, he remained silent, simply gazing at me. Slowly, I endeavored to comfort him, imploring him to share why they're frightening people here.

Eventually, he took hold of my hand and guided me into a room where the rest of the family awaited. It was there that I heard their heartbreaking tale. The woman explained that after her husband's sudden demise from a heart attack, she became the subject of blame and scorn from her own family and villagers. They labeled her a (Shaapit Aurat) harbinger of misfortune, believing that her presence had caused her husband's untimely death. The situation escalated, leading to her unjust expulsion from the village. With nowhere to go, she and her children found this empty villa and made it their home.

I listened closely as they asked for help. Their eyes showed that they hoped for a better life. I was determined to make sure their lives were not filled with fear and loneliness anymore. I reached out to the local police station and even tweeted the government, from whom I didn't get a response unluckily. However, some officers and one archaeologist nearby were dispatched to the Villa, assuming it to be of historical significance.

The family, once living in fear and uncertainty, now looked to me with anticipation. It was clear that they yearned for shelter, sustenance, and a chance at a better life. After this moment, one of the senior officials helped me connecting the Government there, and then with their assistance, I ensured the family was provided with a home and secured a sewing job for the resilient woman at a nearby factory. Their lives were finally imbued with happiness and contentment.

As time passed, the woman began to regard me as family, tying a rakhi around my wrist every year as a symbol of our bond. I, too, found solace in this newfound connection.

This experience taught me a profound lesson that we shouldn't just exist, but live with the realm of life!" It reminded me that life is not meant to be a mechanical routine, but a journey filled with purpose, compassion, and the pursuit of happiness. The magic of emotions and the fulfillment that comes from following our passions and dreams are the very essence of living. And through this, I've learned that pursuing my passion didn't have to be an all-or-nothing endeavor. While the demands of life necessitated a job for financial security, my writing remained an essential part of who I am. It's a means to express my thoughts, challenge societal norms, and ignite conversations that could lead to positive change.

Today, I am here with a new sense of purpose. I continue to balance my responsibilities with my passion for writing, understanding that this is integral to my well-being. I strive to make a difference through my words, awaken minds, and foster a society that is more open-minded, inclusive, and compassionate.

So, let this be a testament to the fact that our passions need not be abandoned in the face of life's demands. Let us remember that true happiness encompasses those interests which stimulate our soul.

I learned that by stepping beyond the boundaries of our comfort zones, we can make a profound difference in the lives of others. The joy I witnessed in the eyes of the once-frightened family became a testament to the power of resilience and the transformative nature of compassion.

Their story serves as a clear reminder that we all have the ability to uplift and support one another. It is through acts of kindness, empathy, and determination that we can bring a new change, transforming lives and weaving a tapestry of shared humanity.

So, my friends, let us not be confined by the monotonous routines of just an existence. Let us embrace the magic of emotions, follow our passions, and work towards turning our dreams into reality. In doing so, we can forge meaningful connections, bring hope into the lives of others, and truly live a life that is rich in purpose and fulfillment.

Remember, each day is an opportunity to make a difference, embrace the extraordinary, and create a legacy of love and compassion. Let's embark on this journey together, hand in hand, with our different stories of joy and the pursuit of living life to its fullest.

Here are some uplifting action steps to embrace that can spark a wave of happiness, helping you live a life that's full and vibrant—beyond just getting by!

1. Discover your Inner Fire: Discover the passions that ignite your soul. Discover things that interest you and make you happy.

2. Embrace the Unknown: Step bravely into the unknown. Embrace new experiences and challenges that stretch your comfort zone, unlocking growth and exhilaration.

3. Cultivate Mindful Gratitude: Embrace mindful gratitude by pausing to appreciate the simple joys and beauty around you. Foster a deep sense of thankfulness for the blessings, both big and small, that enrich your life.

4. Make a Positive Impact: Harness your inner strength to create a positive impact. Show kindness and compassion, and engage in uplifting actions that inspire others.

5. Embody Authenticity: Embrace your true self unapologetically. Celebrate your unique gifts and live authentically by honoring your values and beliefs. Create a life that aligns with your deepest truth.

By taking these positive steps, you can invite a wave of happiness into your life, moving you from just getting by to truly enjoying every moment. Life is all about living it to the fullest and with passion! So, don't just go through the motions—aim to live with purpose and excitement.

Pathways to a Vibrant Life

- Authenticity
- Inner Fire
- Positive Impact
- Unknown
- Mindful Gratitude

**LESSON**:- Keep an eye out for the great opportunities that come your way, chase after your dreams, and remember that you can make a wonderful difference in the world around you!

Chapter - 14
Mental health

POV: - In our fast-paced lives, we experience many different situations that can affect how we feel—whether it's a minor problem, a little accident, or a moment when we feel out of sorts. So, how can we handle these challenges? How does our mind react when things get tough? Taking care of our mental health is becoming increasingly important for everyone. Our feelings, whether we're sad, happy, or stressed, play a big role in how well we can work and enjoy life. Let's take a simple journey together to explore mindfulness and see how it can help improve our mental well-being!

Once, during a meeting, my phone started ringing. It was an unfamiliar number, so I ignored it, thinking it was an unnecessary call. I decided to return the call later, after the meeting. However, a minute later, the phone rang again, and this time, I sensed it might be something important. I excused myself from the meeting for a moment and answered the call. What I heard on call left me losing my mind getting the background blurred in my senses, I was just shocked—my hands started shivering and I became completely still.

The call was from Shimla, where my sister Sarah lived. It was her friend, Kirti, who called to inform me that my sister Sarah had attempted suicide, and they were rushing her to the hospital with the help of nearby people. I abruptly left the meeting and hurried to book a ticket to Shimla. You see, our family consisted of just three people: Sarah, our grandmother, and me.

I arrived in Shimla the same day, my heart overwhelmed with worry about my sister. I rushed to the hospital and anxiously inquired about her condition. The doctor's words were a balm to my worried soul: "Don't worry, your sister is now out of danger." With immense relief, I entered her room. Her eyes were filled with tears as she said, "Sorry, Bhaiya, please forgive me." My initial reaction was a mix of anger, care, and frustration, but above all, I was overjoyed that my sister was safe.

Keeping aside my curiosity about why this happened, I asked the doctor when I could take her home, and he said I could do so by the next morning, following a minor procedure. I felt a great sense of calmness at the prospect of bringing her back to our home.

I brought her home from the serene hills of Shimla, hoping the familiar surroundings would comfort her. Each day, I noticed little changes—her laughter started to bubble up again, and I could see that spark return to her eyes. I was genuinely curious about what had happened, but I also wanted to be sensitive to her feelings. I didn't want to push her if she wasn't ready to share. I just hoped she was finding comfort and joy in being back home. But, On the fourth day after our return, my grandmother and I planned to raise a topic. When the moment felt right, we would ask her about her mental well-being and the reasons behind her drastic step.

As we settled into a cozy spot on the porch, surrounded by the soft chirping of birds and the warm glow of the afternoon sun, I felt the weight of the conversation we needed to have. The discussions about my upcoming marriage had lingered in the air initiated by my grandmother, and it seemed like a good opportunity to check in on her feelings.

With a gentle tone and a caring glance, I turned to her and asked, "What happened, Sarah? What led you to take such a drastic step?" My heart was full of concern, hoping to understand the struggles she'd faced.

She sighed and said, "Mujhe maaf kardo Bhaiya (I'm sorry brother). I was overwhelmed by stress. Anxiety had a tight grip on me, and ever since our parents left us, I've struggled to find mental stability.

You've been doing everything for us, even borrowing money from a friend to pay my registration and examination fees last year. But, I couldn't prepare for the exams, and I felt like I was cheating on you. This guilt made me increasingly frustrated. Then I started losing friends, became withdrawn, and ultimately, I felt like giving up on life." I embraced her warmly and whispered, "Sometimes, it's okay to not be okay, my sister. You're not alone, I'm here for you."

I then took her to meet one of my wonderful friend Sofia, a psychologist, who really helped her understand her needs and provided the right support. It was heartwarming to see how much Sarah improved over time, and it brought us even closer together.

One evening, I met Sofia again, and she shared a startling statistic: one out of every five people is grappling with a mental disorder. This revelation left me shocked.

<u>This experience raised some important questions in my mind that I quickly asked Sofia:</u>

- Why is the Current Generation Experiencing Heightened Mental Health Challenges?

- What factors contribute to the increased prevalence of mental health issues among our generation?

- What should be employed to Improve Mental well-being and Find a Way Out of Mental Health Challenges?

- How can individuals and society as a whole address and overcome the mental health challenges faced by our generation?

After I expressed my curiosity about our generation, Sofia kindly invited me to dinner. During a lovely meal, she took the time to explain everything we would be exploring together, including the significant effects on individuals and the unique challenges we face as a generation. It was truly an enlightening conversation! At last, she also outlined actionable solutions to help us navigate the complexities of mental health and emerge stronger in life.

- *<u>Understanding Mental Health</u>*

1. <u>Mental Health Explained:</u> It's all about how we deal with the ups and downs of life—those unexpected challenges and little mishaps. It's about having the courage to manage stress, nurture our relationships, and face whatever life throws our way. At its heart, mental health is really about our emotional and psychological well-being, and it's important to take care of it!

2. <u>The Continuum of Mental Health:</u> Mental health is not an either/or condition; it exists on a spectrum. At different times, we may find ourselves anywhere along this spectrum, influenced by various factors in our lives.

- *<u>The Impact on Individuals</u>*

1. <u>The Unseen Struggles</u>: Mental health challenges often hide behind a facade of normalcy. Many individuals suffer in silence, fearing judgment or stigma, much like Sarah from this chapter.

2. <u>The Ripple Effect</u>: Mental health issues extend beyond personal struggles. They can disrupt relationships, hamper career growth, and diminish overall quality of life. Recognizing this impact is crucial to understanding the importance of addressing it.

Mental health disorders do not discriminate based on age, gender, income, or ethnicity; they can affect anyone, highlighting the universal nature of this risk. A person's mental health can be influenced by a variety of factors, including their social or financial circumstances, adverse childhood experiences, biological traits, and underlying medical conditions.

Furthermore, it's crucial to recognize that individuals with mental health disorders often experience multiple conditions simultaneously.

It's important to recognize that good mental health is influenced by a mix of different factors. Many things can contribute to the development of mental health issues. For instance, ongoing social and economic pressures can create tough situations. People facing financial challenges or belonging to marginalized ethnic groups may be more likely to experience these struggles.

Additionally, childhood experiences play a big role in our mental well-being. Studies have shown that difficult times in childhood, like abuse, the loss of a parent, or a parent's illness, can have lasting effects as we grow older. There's a lot more to this topic, but understanding these connections is a great start in supporting mental health!

Still, many people don't take it seriously when a person suffers from mental traumas. And if we take a look at reports, then we'll get to know that Mental health issues impact a lot of people. About 19% of adults, 46% of teenagers, and 13% of kids (data taken from Google) experience mental trauma every year. This means that someone you know, like a family member, neighbor, teacher, coworker, or someone at your place of worship, might be going through a tough time with their mental health.

However, there's a significant problem: only about half of those struggling with mental health receive the help they need. A major reason for this is the pervasive shame and embarrassment surrounding mental health issues. When individuals don't seek the necessary support, it can lead to a range of adverse consequences, including more disruptive situations, increased medical expenses, poor performance in school or work, greater difficulty in finding employment, and, unfortunately, a heightened risk of self-harm.

If you've watched the movie 3 Idiots, the leading character Rancho from the movie once said, "Engineers are quite clever; they've created machines to measure physical pressure, but there is no way to measure the pressure that builds in the mind." Currently, there are no specific tests or scans that can definitively diagnose mental illnesses.

However, we can be aware with the help of some signs that people develop generally when they suffer from a traumatic phase in life, and those signs are:

- Social Isolation: When someone starts pulling away from friends, family, or co-workers.

- Loss of Interest: If they stop enjoying activities they used to love.

- Sleep Changes: Noticeable shifts in their sleep patterns, either sleeping too much or too little.

- Appetite Shifts: Eating habits that drastically change, whether overeating or not eating enough.

- Hopelessness: When they seem to be losing hope or feeling very down.

- Low Energy: Consistently having low energy levels and feeling drained.

- Increased Substance Use: Using substances like alcohol or nicotine more frequently to cope.

- Negative Emotions: Displaying a lot of negative emotions like sadness or anger.

- Confusion: Being noticeably confused or disoriented.

- <u>Difficulty with Daily Tasks:</u> Struggling to do everyday things like going to work or preparing a meal.

- <u>Intrusive Thoughts:</u> Persistent thoughts or memories that keep coming back.

- <u>Self-Harm or Harm to Others:</u> Expressing thoughts of hurting themselves or someone else.

- <u>Auditory Hallucinations:</u> Hearing voices that others don't hear.

- <u>Delusional Beliefs:</u> Experiencing beliefs that don't align with reality.

Being aware of these signs can help you support someone who may be going through a challenging time with their mental health.

We've to break the silence surrounding mental health. Engaging in open, non-judgmental conversations and challenging societal stigma to encourage more people to come forward to seek help.

Certainly! There's an important factor that plays a big role in our mental well-being, and that's the environment we find ourselves in. This includes not just our surroundings, but also the people we spend our time with, our daily routines, and how others perceive us.

<u>Think about it:</u> A child growing up in a loving family often absorbs and reflects the values and perspectives of their home. On the other hand, a child who moves away from their parental home might start to rely more on the influences of their immediate environment. This happens because about half of how we live our lives comes from what we see and learn from those around us. It's amazing how much our surroundings can shape our outlook on life, isn't it?

<u>I'm thrilled to present an engaging checklist inspired by the key lessons from this chapter on mental health. This guide</u>

will empower you to infuse positivity into your daily life and enhance your well-being! Let's get started!

1. <u>Self-Reflection</u>: Take some time to reflect on your mental well-being. Are there any signs of stress or anxiety in your life that you've been ignoring?

2. <u>Open Communication</u>: Encourage open and honest conversations about mental health with your friends and family. Check-in on their well-being and let them know you're there to support them.

3. <u>Awareness</u>: Learn about the signs of mental health issues. Understanding these signs can help you see when someone might need help.

4. <u>Challenge Stigma</u>: Challenge societal stigma surrounding mental health. Be a part of the solution by promoting understanding and empathy instead of judgment.

5. <u>Support System</u>: Build and nurture a strong support system of friends and loved ones who can provide emotional assistance during tough times.

6. <u>Seek Professional Help</u>: If you or someone you know is facing mental health challenges, don't hesitate to seek professional help. Reach out to a mental health expert who can provide guidance and treatment.

7. <u>Create a Positive Environment</u>: Pay attention to your surroundings and the people you interact with regularly. Strive to create a positive and supportive environment that promotes mental well-being.

Mental Health Checklist

**LESSON**: - *Don't forget to share your compassion with those in need and recognize the importance of understanding the mental well-being of your loved ones. By doing so, we can individually contribute to creating positive change. Enjoy your reading!*

Chapter - 15
Suicidal thoughts

POV: - "Ever come across a person who somehow has lost all hope?" It's a heavy feeling, and we all know that suicide rates are increasing daily. But do we truly understand why someone would consider giving up on life? In this chapter, we will compassionately explore the difficult topic of suicide. Through stories and thoughtful insights, we aim to understand the minds of struggling people and offer support. Let's approach this with kindness, as acknowledging these challenges can help us find ways to extend a helping hand.

In quiet moments, when sadness feels like too much and darkness seems to close in around us, we often come across a topic that many choose to keep hidden. It's something really important for all of us to understand: our mental health.

Welcome to "Unraveling the Darkness: Understanding Suicidal Thoughts." This chapter takes us on a journey into the deep struggles of those dealing with overwhelming sadness, with the hope of shedding light on this difficult topic related to mental health.

<u>Picture this:</u> One quick choice might decide if someone lives or dies. As you turn the pages, we ask you to stay a little longer because, in these words, we may have the potential to alter destinies.

In life we've two aspects to take care of, one is our physical fitness and another one is our mental health. We all know that it's really important to pay attention to both our physical fitness along with our mental well-being! Many of us hit the gym and try to eat healthy to keep our bodies in shape which is really good, but when it comes to taking care of our mental well-being, we sometimes struggle. We might start feeling a bit low, and our energy can dip over time. Instead of addressing those feelings, we might find ourselves giving up or falling into some unhealthy habits to escape or suppress those mental challenges temporarily. While these habits might give us a little relief at the moment, they often end up affecting both our mental and physical health in the long run.

Mental health can be really complex, and one of the hardest things to deal with is having thoughts of suicide. This section isn't just about gaining knowledge; it's about helping to save lives. For too long, shame has kept people from talking about their suicidal feelings and seeking the help they need. It's important to break that silence and encourage open conversations.

In the pages ahead, our mission is clear: to shed light on the profound and often perplexing issue of suicidal thoughts. Our goal is to empower both those who may be battling these thoughts and those who wish to support them.

As we move through this chapter, we'll be revealing the complex layers of suicidal thoughts, the warning signs to look for, and the ways to address and prevent them.

Before we proceed, let's pause for a minute and reflect. Have you, or someone close to you, ever grappled with these thoughts? Have you contemplated the depths of despair or reached out to someone who has? As you read on, let these questions guide your engagement with the content, for it is not only about awareness but also about compassion.

The numbers paint a grim picture. According to recent data, suicide has become the leading cause of death globally. The statistics underscore the urgency of this issue. This chapter is not just an exploration; it is a call to action.

Have you ever seen someone who seems to be struggling and feels like giving up on life? It's a tough topic, and we often hear about how mental health issues affect not just regular people but also famous figures. Some of these celebrities have even tried to take their own lives. But do we really understand what's going on in their minds? What leads them to feel like they have no other option but to give up?

Absolutely! There are so many reasons we might not grasp the pain others are experiencing, and it's tough to understand what they're going through. But no matter what, we can find the strength to embrace life again.

When someone is going through really tough emotional times, they might start to have thoughts about wanting to end their life. This can happen due to a variety of reasons, like feeling very sad, facing a lot of stress, or feeling hopeless. Different situations, such as deep depression, past traumas, ongoing health issues, or struggles with drugs and alcohol, can all play a part in these feelings. It's important to keep in mind that everyone's experience is different, and there isn't just one reason why someone might feel this way. If you or someone you know is having these thoughts, it's really important to talk to someone who can help.

Here I'm continuing the next stage of this chapter with a heartwarming story. The Story of a Friend's Lifeline: The Story of Raj and Abhinav

In the heart of Delhi, two close friends, Raj and Abhinav, shared a strong friendship built on years of laughter, dreams, and many late-night talks. However, everything changed when Abhinav faced a tough time that left him feeling lost and heartbroken.

Abhinav had been in a loving relationship with his girlfriend for nearly ten years. Their story was one that many people admired. They were close, shared dreams for the future, and planned to get married soon. But then, unexpectedly, their relationship ended. Abhinav's heart was broken, and his world fell apart.

The pain he felt was overwhelming. It was like an emotional storm inside him, tearing at his soul. He experienced deep emotional trauma and filled his mind with memories of his time with his girlfriend. This led him to consider a terrible choice: ending his own life. The weight of his feelings felt too heavy, and he thought he had nowhere to turn.

Meanwhile, in Bangalore, Raj was planning a surprise visit. He knew about Abhinav's heartache and understood that his friend needed support. Raj decided to visit Abhinav to show him he was not alone in this difficult time.

When Raj arrived, he hugged Abhinav with a smile but noticed a significant change in him. Abhinav, who used to be full of life, now seemed like a shadow of his former self. His eyes, once bright with hope, now showed deep sadness.

Raj felt heartbroken seeing his friend suffer. Determined to help, he spent hours talking with Abhinav, trying to understand his feelings. With patience and a listening ear, Raj supported his friend. Slowly, Abhinav began to feel a little better and showed signs of moving forward.

One evening, as Raj was preparing for an urgent meeting in Delhi, he took a moment to write a warm letter to Abhinav. He wanted to share some words of encouragement, something that Abhinav could hold onto during the hard days. The letter was filled with positivity and hope, reminding his friend that brighter days were ahead.

How about checking out that heartfelt letter written to a best friend who's going through a tough time? It's amazing how one little note from a friend can open someone's eyes to the beauty and importance of life, even during the hardest moments.

Here is the letter:

Dear Abhinav,

You know you're a Rising Star. Have you ever thought about why you're here on this beautiful Earth? It's incredible to consider the love your mom felt for you during those nine months as she waited for your arrival. She faced challenges and pain, all because she wanted to embrace you and share the love of the universe with you.

I know you haven't talked much about the tough times you're facing, but your mom has reached out to me. She's really worried about you and just wants to help during this tough period. I could feel how emotional she was when we spoke; she's concerned that showing her feelings in front of you might make things harder for you. Just remember, you are her only child, and you mean a lot to her. She was really hoping to come to visit you for a few days, but you had denied it, mentioning that you'd be away in another city for a meeting.

You may already know that once doctors told your mother that she might never have a child, but after many prayers, you came into her life—that's something truly beautiful. I can't say anything about your girlfriend and the value you kept in her life, but I can tell you this: To your mom, you are her shining light and source of hope. You matter so much to her!

You being here means you have a purpose, even if you don't fully grasp its significance. Have you ever considered your father's dreams of holding your hand, feeling your love, and having your support when he grows old? Have you thought about your parents' smiles and the voice of your mother asking you "Beta, tu thik hai na"?

These things might seem less important at times, but they hold deep meaning. Your life is not just your own; it's connected to many hearts, and it serves a purpose.

Often, when something bad happens or someone hurts us, we start thinking about giving up. But have you ever thought about the people who care about you, who love you, and want you in their lives?

I know you are in severe pain and of course, you'll have to suffer from it because you had the deepest emotional connection with the person you have given all your heart to, I know how much you've loved her and how a heartbreak completely shatters a person from the innermost feeling of losing hope. But, is giving up the right response to life's challenges? Have you considered how your parents would feel if they knew that their love, support, and care had been in vain because you gave up when life got tough?

Life is a mix of emotions, situations, and experiences we can't predict. Sometimes, even the Almighty tests our strength and love for our dear ones. We must face what life throws at us. It's through facing problems and finding solutions that we become stronger.

Sometimes, life can be really overwhelming, and it might feel like giving up is the only option. But it's important to remember that the strength you have from your family and the courage inside you can carry you through tough times. Your life belongs to you, and the choices you make to face your challenges shape your journey.

There are solutions for everything, so don't let your mind dwell on giving up. It has the power to influence others and remember that ending it could harm more lives.

Here, we've to understand that if you have the power to tackle a problem, why worry? But if it's beyond your control, move forward, as life has much more to offer. I know you might be thinking that these are very easy for me to say but this is the only way, my friend. Your life has a purpose; if you're alive, it's because the Almighty has plans for you. No matter how big your problems seem, remember that giving up won't solve them. It may only make things worse and hurt the lives connected to yours.

For the sake of your loved ones, your parents, and the plans the Almighty has for you, never give up. You deserve love, and your presence serves a purpose. I call you a rising star because I believe you'll shine brightly someday.

Here's a little suggestion for you! If you're experiencing any emotions—whether it's happiness, sadness, or something else—why not write it down in a diary? You could even save a page for someone you really care about, like a special friend or family member, to share your thoughts with, even if you feel shy about doing it directly. And just so you know, if you ever want to talk, I'm here to listen! Writing can be a great way to express what you're feeling, especially on days when talking to others seems hard. Give it a go!

You can call me or come to meet me whenever you need, now I've to go, but I'm assuring you that we'll meet again soon, just be hopeful.

Sending you warm hugs, hope, and light. Remember, no matter what the situation is, suicide is never the answer.

Stay strong, my friend.

With care and support,

Raj

After reading the heartfelt letter that Raj left for him before taking leave, Abhinav came to a beautiful realization: his life was meaningful, not just for himself, but also for the many people who genuinely cared about him.

As he absorbed Raj's words, a light burst through the darkness clouding Abhinav's mind. He recognized that love and hope were still present in his life, and he didn't have to face his struggles alone.

In the days, weeks, and months that followed, Raj remained a true source of comfort for Abhinav. He encouraged him to seek out professional help and stood by him every step of the way. Slowly but surely, with Raj's steadfast support and the love of other loved ones, Abhinav began to heal.

This story highlights the incredible power of friendship, love, and compassion during life's toughest times. It's a reminder that no one should ever feel to suffer it being silent. Sometimes, just reaching out to a friend can make all the difference. With Raj's help and the support of those who loved him, Abhinav started to find his way back to brighter days.

Remember, even in the darkest moments, there's always hope and support available—in the form of a caring friend or a loved one or sometimes even as a stranger.

One day, while I was deep into writing this chapter, I had a chat with my friend Dr. Swati Shukla, a psychologist who is always so insightful. When I mentioned I was working on a piece about how people deal with tough times, she perked up with interest! Our conversation blossomed into a fascinating discussion about the different mindsets she encounters in her practice. It lasted almost an hour, and during that time, she shared stories about how sometimes, she feels at a bit of a loss for words when she hears people open up about their struggles.

Dr. Shukla also touched on a serious topic: each year, a significant number of people lose their lives to suicide. Sadly, many of these tragedies arise from the complex workings of the human mind. She pointed out that few individuals speak out about their feelings, and when emotional pain becomes overwhelming, some may even think about ending their lives.

She emphasized how important it is to seek professional help right away if someone is experiencing intense emotional pain or having thoughts of self-harm or suicide. While she offers helpful advice, she made it clear that it's crucial to recognize when it's urgent to turn to a professional for support.

She also shared a friendly suggestion for anyone going through a tough time emotionally.

- <u>Reach Out to a Mental Health Professional:</u> A licensed therapist, counselor, or psychiatrist can provide you with the necessary guidance and support. They are trained to help individuals navigate through intense emotional pain.

- <u>Confide in a Trusted Friend or Family Member:</u> Sharing your feelings with someone you trust can be an immense relief. Friends and family can provide emotional support and may encourage you to seek professional help.

- <u>Call a Helpline:</u> There are numerous crisis helplines available 24/7. These lines are staffed with trained professionals who can offer immediate support.

Here are some helpline numbers in India for mental health crises:

1. Arpita Suicide Prevention Helpline: 080-23655557, Monday to Friday, 10 AM–1 PM and 2–5 PM

2. Voice That Cares (ROCF): 8448-8448-45, 7 days a week, 9 AM–9 PM

3. Aasra: +91-9820466726, available 24 hours a day, 7 days a week

4. Connecting Trust: +91-9922001122 or +91-9922004305, available 12 PM–8 PM, 7 days a week

5. COOJ Mental Health Foundation: +91-832-2252525, available weekdays, 1 PM–7 PM

(Source: - Google)

I wish you all the best and hope you're doing well in life. But, if you ever feel like giving up or notice someone struggling with these feelings, please consider following these important steps:

- <u>Limit Access to Means:</u> If possible, remove any means of self-harm or suicide from your immediate environment. This may include medications, firearms, or other potentially dangerous items.

- Avoid Isolation: Isolating yourself can intensify emotional pain. Try to stay connected with friends and family, even if it's difficult.

- Practice Self-Care: Engage in self-care activities that help reduce emotional distress. This may be exercising or meditating, journaling, or pursuing hobbies.

- Stay Away from Alcohol and Drugs: Substance abuse can make emotional pain worse and cloud your judgment. It's best to avoid these substances when you're feeling vulnerable.

- Set Short-Term Goals: Sometimes, breaking down life into smaller, manageable goals can provide a sense of relief and accomplishment.

- Know That Feelings Can Change: Remember that intense emotional pain is often temporary. Even though it may seem endless, it can improve with time and professional help.

- Accept Support: Allow others to help you. Opening up to support doesn't make you weak; it shows strength in seeking help and finding solutions.

- Create a Safety Plan: Develop a safety plan with your mental health professional or counselor. This plan outlines steps to take when you experience thoughts of self-harm or suicide.

It's really important to pay attention to any thoughts of hurting yourself or feeling like you want to end your life. Getting help from a professional is essential, and there are many people and resources available to support you during tough times. You don't have to face this alone; there is hope for feeling better and healing.

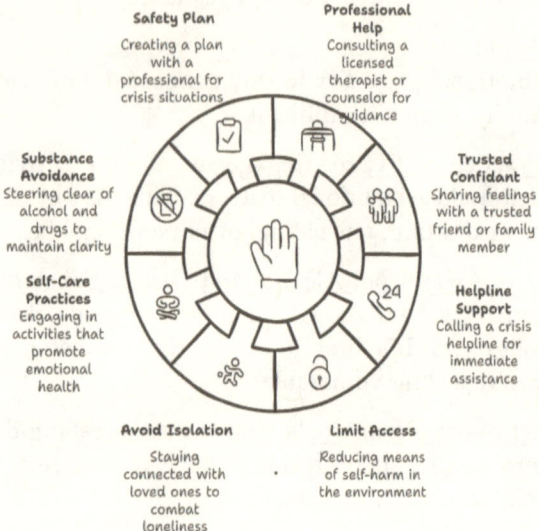

Strategies for Emotional Well-Being

Safety Plan — Creating a plan with a professional for crisis situations

Professional Help — Consulting a licensed therapist or counselor for guidance

Substance Avoidance — Steering clear of alcohol and drugs to maintain clarity

Trusted Confidant — Sharing feelings with a trusted friend or family member

Self-Care Practices — Engaging in activities that promote emotional health

Helpline Support — Calling a crisis helpline for immediate assistance

Avoid Isolation — Staying connected with loved ones to combat loneliness

Limit Access — Reducing means of self-harm in the environment

LESSON: Remember, your life has value, and seeking help is a sign of strength, not weakness. You are not alone in your struggles; there is hope for healing and recovery. Reach out, confide in someone, and let the support of others guide you through the darkest moments.

Chapter - 16
The social media life

POV: - The social media life—yes, I'm talking about the life we live online, the way we present our personalities there! Have you ever gone out for a meal with friends or family? I think almost we've all been sometimes! What's the first thing you do when you arrive? Many of us snap a photo, right? It's completely okay to save your memories by taking a snap. Today, it's so easy to get caught up in capturing the moment or scrolling through our phones instead of really enjoying that time with people we care about. In today's world, we've created this whole second life online through our social media accounts. But have you ever wondered whether the people you follow are really as happy as they seem? Do they genuinely enjoy their lives, or are they just putting on a show? It's important to take a moment to reflect on the images of happiness and success we share online. So, let's take a little journey together to explore our online selves. Are we truly living up to the way we present ourselves on social media? It could be an eye-opening experience!

Once I was at the gym, feeling the rhythm of my feet hitting the treadmill as I immersed myself in my workout. After a few minutes, I noticed a girl stepping onto the treadmill right next to me. She started her machine but ran for even less than a minute. Then, to my surprise, she quickly pulled out her phone and began snapping photos, her face lit up with excitement.

Curious about her sudden exit from running, I turned to her and asked curiously if she was done already. With a cheerful grin, she replied, "Oh, I'm not really here to run—I just wanted to capture some cool pictures for my social media account!"

In a world increasingly connected by the digital threads of the internet, we find ourselves navigating a new realm of existence: The Social Media Life. This chapter invites you to explore the profound impact of social platforms on our daily experiences, relationships, self-identity, and even our understanding of reality. Together, we'll delve into the complexities and opportunities of our online lives, dissecting the evolution of this digital landscape and the profound ways it shapes our world.

Friends, we can observe in today's digital age, social media, like Snapchat, Instagram, Facebook, and Twitter, has reshaped our notion of beauty. We've transitioned from using makeup to enhance our looks to crafting idealized online personas. But is social media just about beauty? I think now it has become a stage for self-expression. We share happiness, achievements, and wealth, projecting a curated image. The challenge lies in maintaining authenticity and resisting the pressure to behave in the same way as most other people in a group or society are behaving. This chapter champions self-awareness and growth, revealing that despite our online facades, inner struggles persist. It encourages us to heal these wounds, emphasizing the importance of sharing experiences and genuine connections in an often superficial digital world.

You'll fall into the depths of the online platforms and reality at every step of reading. We'll move by taking our view stepwise on this matter.

The Digital Persona vs. Real-Life Identity:

Here we'll explore some important yet often overlooked aspects of our online lives on social media. Understanding these small details can really make a difference in how we interact and connect in today's digital world!

Online vs. Real: How We Act on Social Media

Have you ever noticed how people act one way online and a different way in real life? It's like they have two versions of themselves. Let's talk about why this happens and what it does to how they feel about themselves and their relationships.

On social media, folks like to show off a cooler version of themselves. It's like they pick and choose the best parts to share. Maybe they do it to get more likes or seem more interesting. It's not always the same as how they are in real life.

Then Why Are People Doing This?

There can be different reasons. Some want everyone to like them like an attention seeker, so they share the coolest stuff. Others are worried about not fitting in, so they act in a way they think others will like. It's like they're putting on a show to get attention.

Feeling a Little Blue Sometimes? You're Not Alone!

You know, sometimes when we get caught up in trying to look cool online, it can leave us feeling a bit down. Have you ever found yourself checking for likes and comments after posting a special moment or a fun photo on social media? It's easy to think we have to measure up to what everyone else is sharing. Plus, scrolling through everyone's highlight reels can make us sometimes question how we feel about ourselves.

It's important to remember that these posts often only show the happy side of people's lives—their successes, their best moments, and even a little fiction sometimes! You rarely see the behind-the-scenes struggles, the arguments with loved ones, or the hard work that goes into those great parties.

So, let's keep in mind that we all have our ups and downs in our own unique ways, and that's perfectly okay! Embrace your journey, and remember you're not alone in how you feel!

Keeping It Real:

While being cool online is definitely a blast, it's super important to just be yourself! When you showcase the real you, both online and in person, you open the door to genuine friendships. It's like saying, "Hey, this is me—consider it or leave it!" Building connections that are based on authenticity instead of just a shiny online persona really makes our friendships stronger.

FOMO and Social Comparison:

Let's talk about FOMO and social media. FOMO means "Fear of Missing Out." It's that vibe you get when you see other people having a blast on social media, and you start stressing that you're missing out on all the fun. This happens a lot because social media often shows the best parts of people's lives.

Imagine scrolling through Instagram, and everyone seems to have perfect lives — exciting vacations, fancy meals, and fun events. Seeing this all the time can make you feel like your own life isn't as cool. It might even make you anxious or like you're not doing enough.

Real data shows that many people feel the same. Studies signify that spending too much time on social media can make FOMO worse. So, it's essential to remember that what you see online is just a part of someone's life, not the whole story. Taking breaks from social media and focusing on your own experiences can help beat that FOMO feeling.

The Influence of Influencers:

Let's have a look into the world of social media influencers, those folks who share their lives online and have a big impact on what we buy, what's cool, and sometimes even what we think about our relationships or politics. We'll see how they influence us, the good and not-so-good stuff, and the responsibilities that come with being an influencer.

A Quick question – have you ever turned to your favorite influencers before making a decision or finalizing any product in your shopping cart? Whether it's about buying cool stuff or shaping your thoughts, influencers in the digital era play a big role. I bet most of you nodded along! They're like the trendsetters of today, influencing what we wear, buy, and sometimes even how we think about our relationships or politics. Yep, you heard it right – politics! But, hold on a second. What about the ethics? Sometimes, influencers get paid to promote things, and they might not spill the beans. About 70% of people think influencers should be upfront about getting paid. It's like being honest with your pals about why you're suggesting something. Having tons of followers is awesome, no doubt, but it comes with responsibilities. Influencers can sway opinions, so they need to be mindful of what they say. More than 80% of young folks think influencers should use their platform for good things. It's like having this superpower, and you have to be smart about how you use it.

They have an incredible impact on our activities. They're the cool trendsetters and sometimes even our political compass. But, here's the deal – with great power comes greater responsibility. Being transparent about promotions and using influence for good is a must. So, as we cruise through this influencer-packed world, let's remember the power they hold and the responsibilities that come with it. Pretty cool, don't you think?

Mental Health and Social Media:

In today's digital age, where social media is a big part of our lives, it's crucial to talk about how it affects our mental health. Spending too much time on social media can lead to problems like addiction, anxiety, and sometimes depression. Recent studies show that excessive use of platforms like Facebook and Instagram is linked to feelings of loneliness and low self-esteem. It's like a loop – you spend more time online, and it can make you feel worse about yourself.

But here's the good news – there are ways to tackle this. Taking breaks from social media, setting time limits, and being mindful of how much you use it can make a big difference. Connecting with friends in real life and doing activities offline also play a role in keeping our mental health in check. It's all about finding a balance. So, while social media is fun and helps us stay connected, it's crucial to be aware of how it affects our mental well-being and take steps to keep it in check. After all, a healthy mind is just as important as staying connected online!

<u>Online Activism and Social Change:</u>

In the world of social media, there's more than just sharing photos and videos. It is a very powerful tool for activism and change-making. A great example is the #BlackLivesMatter movement, which started on social media and grew into a global call for justice against racial inequality. Similarly, the #MeToo movement gained momentum as people shared their stories on platforms like Twitter, shining a light on the issue of sexual harassment. Social media played a crucial role in the Arab Spring too, where people in the Middle East used platforms like Facebook to organize and voice their demands for political change. These movements show that social media isn't just about likes and shares; it can be a force for positive change and a platform for voices that need to be heard. It's like turning a digital space into a stage for real-world impact!

<u>The Dark Side of Social Media:</u>

Are you aware of how people today leak private pictures online? There are many applications and websites, which are often used for malicious purposes. You may have also heard about cases where someone's private pictures went viral, which is completely unacceptable and often done in the name of entertainment.

Many individuals try to manipulate others through chats and video calls. Once you accept their call, they may provoke you into revealing your face, and then they might blackmail you—demanding money or threatening to share the footage, either edited or manipulated, in a compromising manner. Even many celebrities have faced such issues.

I know that the government has implemented various measures to address these problems, but we must also take personal responsibility for our safety. It's important to recognize that our security ultimately lies in our own hands.

As we know, every advantage comes with its drawbacks, and social media is no exception, presenting some darker consequences. In the big world of social media, many unacceptable pieces of stuff are deteriorating people's lives consistently, like cyberbullying, online harassment, and people spreading hate. These are like dark shadows on the internet that can make people feel really bad. Did you know that approximately 37% of young people aged 12 to 17 in India have been bullied online? This issue isn't limited to India; around 41% of adults in the United States have experienced online harassment, with 25% of them encountering more severe forms of harassment.

It's a big problem. Online harassment is another issue. Shockingly, more than half of adults, around 53%, have faced online harassment. Social media gives people a way to be mean to others without showing who they are, which makes it even more challenging.

Hate speech is also on the rise, spreading negativity and dividing people. Recent studies show a worrying 64% increase in hate speech in the past year. This is not good for anyone using social media. Stopping these problems is hard because there's so much content online, and it's tough to find and remove the bad stuff quickly. Social media platforms try to figure out how to let people express themselves while also keeping users safe. It's like walking a tightrope.

To make social media a better place, everyone needs to work together. Platforms need good rules, people need to be aware of how they treat others online, and technology needs to help too. By creating a kind and understanding online culture, we can make sure social media stays a positive space for everyone.

The Economics of Social Media:

Let's talk about the money side of social media. Social media isn't just about connecting with friends; it's also a big business. One way these platforms make money is through advertising. Companies pay social media sites, big influencers, and celebrities to show their ads to users. Did you know that social media ad spending is expected to reach around $165 billion in a year? That's huge!

Now, about those people who post cool stuff and have a ton of followers – they're called influencers. These influencers also make great money. Companies pay them to promote their products. Many of them even make a living out of it. The whole business of influencers is booming, and it's expected to reach $15 billion by next year.

So, why does this matter for the economy? Well, all this money flowing through social media creates jobs. From content creators to advertising experts, many people find work in the digital space. This digital age has opened up new opportunities, making it an exciting time for those who understand the ins and outs of social media. As we scroll through our feeds, it's good to remember that behind those posts and ads, there's a whole economy at play. It would be beneficial if you developed an interest or possessed knowledge in understanding the economic and financial aspects of social media, facilitating exponential growth.

Here are some insightful to-do lists for individuals genuinely seeking valuable takeaways from this chapter:

1. **Stay Authentic:** In the digital world, staying true to who you are matters. Be genuine in both your online and offline life, fostering real connections based on authenticity.

2. **Balance Online Coolness with Reality:** While it's fun to showcase the cool parts of your life online, remember to keep it real. Balancing your online persona with your true self helps maintain a healthy relationship with the connections we have online and offline.

3. **Combat FOMO with Reality Checks:** Feeling the Fear of Missing Out (FOMO)? Take breaks from social media, and remember that what you see online is just a small glimpse of someone's life. Focus on your own experiences and appreciate the present.

4. **Influence Wisely:** If you're an influencer or looking up to one, remember the power they hold. Be transparent about promotions, use your influence for good, and consider the impact your words can have on others.

5. **Prioritize Mental Health:** Excessive social media use can impact mental health. Set time limits, take breaks, and engage in offline activities to find the right balance. Your mental well-being is crucial.

6. **Use Social Media for Positive Change:** Explore the power of social media beyond likes and shares. Participate in movements for social change, amplify voices that need to be heard, and contribute to a positive online environment.

7. **Combat Cyberbullying and Online Harassment:** Be careful to whom you open, aware of the dark side of social media. Report it if you witness any cyberbullying or harassment. Create a comfortable online culture and

promote understanding to make social media a safe space for everyone.

8. <u>Understand the Economics of Social Media:</u> Recognize the business side of social media. Understand how advertising works, acknowledge the influence of influencers, and grasp the economic opportunities the digital age offers.

9. <u>Stay Informed about Privacy:</u> Protect your privacy online. Be cautious about with whom you're sharing personal information and pics and stay informed about the consequences of data breaches.

LESSON:- Keep your privacy in preference while navigating social media. Work together to make this space safe and enjoyable for everyone. Remember, it's easy to fall into the FOMO trap when you see others' highlights, but everyone has their own journey. Enjoy your time online!

Chapter - 17
Dreams & determination

POV: - Have you ever felt like giving up on your dreams and doing something that you never thought of? Maybe life took you in a direction far from what you once thought would be your big achievements. Here, many people have created a perception that if something doesn't seem good or in a favorable way then they start blaming their luck, their desires, or whatnot. I want us to look back not to make you sad or guilty about the past, but to realize that it's not always just luck that decides our success. Many times, it's about having a strong determination and the belief that you should never settle for anything less. Let's explore this idea in this chapter, understanding that everyone, at some point, faces a reality that goes beyond what we think, always urging us to stay determined.

In our world, it's not uncommon for people to let go of their dreams and settle for an ordinary life. Many have faced situations where they end up doing things they never really wanted to do—jobs that are just okay, not the ones they truly wanted. Have you ever met someone like that? Sure, we've all been in situations where we either encounter people facing these struggles, or we ourselves find that what we're doing isn't what we really wanted. It's something many can relate to—the realization that we might be on a path that doesn't align with our original thoughts and plans.

Many people you encounter may be pursuing paths that differ significantly from their original life goals. In fact, if you engage in conversation with those around you, you might discover that most of them are not following their true dreams. This reality can be painful, as it often stems from individuals giving up on their aspirations, experiencing too many setbacks, or lacking the opportunities necessary to chase what they genuinely desire.

Alright, let me break it down for you:

Have you ever heard of determination? It's a powerful feeling that helps us perform well, even in challenging situations. People who possess determination often gain recognition for their outstanding achievements in their careers or fields. Today, let's explore this concept further. What does "determination" mean to you? Is it about working hard, being consistent, or something else?

Well, guess what? It's not just one thing. Different people see it in different ways. Determination is like climbing a mountain. Each step requires effort, and sometimes the path is steep and rocky. Along the way, climbers must make decisions about the best route, rely on others for guidance, and adapt to challenges. Just like a climber who pushes through fatigue and obstacles to reach the summit, individuals committed to their dreams persist through difficulties in pursuit of their goals, whether it's a stable job, an artistic masterpiece, or implementing your ideas into a form of startup and making it a unicorn.

So, step one: think about what you really want in life, and then you'll find out how determined you can be. Right?

Choosing Average: A Common Challenge

We've all seen it—people giving up on their dreams and settling for a regular, average life. They take jobs that don't excite them and accept salaries that don't really show how valuable they are. Many people find themselves doing something far from what they once dreamed of, and it happens a lot.

Have you ever asked yourself why things end up this way? Well, it's usually because we lose our determination, and faith, and get weighed down by a lot of responsibilities. Nowadays, if someone wants to chase their dream, they often have to listen to what society and people around them say. Unfortunately, these folks might bring us down, telling us to forget about our dreams, insisting, "There's nothing valuable in those pursuits."

"Have you ever heard a line: 'Follow your dreams so hard that others start dreaming about hanging out with you?' True!" Take a moment to think, and you might realize you know someone like that. You can also find some examples even around you.

We often invest our all into the things we love, but sometimes things do not go as planned. But that doesn't mean we failed, rather, it should be viewed as a learning experience—an opportunity to recalibrate our approach. we need to see the moment just like an unsuccessful attempt. It's just a bump on the road, and there are always lots of chances to try again.

Pursuing opportunities is like fishing in a vast ocean. There are countless fish (opportunities) waiting to be caught, but you need the right bait (passion and effort) and the willingness to cast your line (take action) to reel them in. If you just sit on the shore and wait, you might miss out on a big catch!

There are two kinds of people: those who let society influence them and stick to the safe path, like staying in a job without seeking further growth because society says it's safer that way. The second one is those who don't let other people or factors hold them back. They go after their dreams and grab every opportunity that comes their way. These are the people who always want more and work hard to achieve their goals. So, start by figuring out what kind of person you are and what you truly want to be.

Remember, you can always try again and keep going! Failing only occurs if you give up. In this world, there are all sorts of people with different ways of thinking. You have to find what makes you truly happy and satisfied.

Whether you're a student, an entrepreneur, or doing a salaried job, it's important to have a clear goal and be committed to achieving it in life. For this, your success will depend on how determined you are.

Achieving a dream requires not only vision but also determination, and it won't be easy. Start by envisioning the worst-case scenario: what if you give your all to pursue your dream and it doesn't succeed? Then, consider the best possible outcomes that could arise from your efforts. Take your time to reflect and ask yourself if you're ready to confront the challenges that may arise in pursuit of the best results. This journey might involve losing some relationships and experiencing opportunity costs, depending on your circumstances. Once you've made your decision, give it your all! You'll find that your determination and hard work will lead you to the answers you're looking for. You've got this!

Here's insights and the to-do list for Genuine Seekers:

1. Reflect on whether you've accepted an ordinary life or if you're actively pursuing your goals.

2. Consider your dreams and evaluate the opportunity costs that you have to bear.

3. Identify any societal influences or external pressures that may be holding you back from pursuing your dreams.

4. Assess your readiness to confront challenges and setbacks to achieve your desired outcomes.

5. Commit to prioritizing your dreams and take proactive steps to make them your reality.

<u>**LESSON**</u>: - Achieving your dreams is much like climbing a mountain. Just as a climber doesn't give up despite slips and setbacks, staying committed to your goals can lead to a breathtaking view of success at the top.

Chapter - 18
Satisfaction & its enormous feeling

POV: - Hey there! Have you ever thought about what satisfaction really means? We often believe that once we achieve certain goals—a dream job, a perfect partner, or something else—we will finally feel satisfied. But have you stopped to wonder if those things will genuinely make you happy in the long run? Or are they merely temporary pleasures that we mistake for true satisfaction?

In this chapter, let's take a closer look at the concepts of satisfaction and happiness. We will explore whether the things we desire are genuinely satisfying or just fleeting pleasures. It's time to dive deep and uncover the truth about what truly brings satisfaction in life.

Imagine this: You're a child, and every day without fail, your dad gives you a ten rupee note as your pocket money. It's a comforting routine that brings you joy. However, one day your dad says, "Let's go to school, son. I'll give you your pocket money there." Excited, you agree, looking forward to that familiar ten rupee note. But when you arrive at school, you discover that your dad's wallet is empty of ten-rupee notes, and all he has are some coins totaling seven rupees. Suddenly, your heart sinks. You're filled with disappointment, maybe even a bit of betrayal. Why? Because you've grown accustomed to receiving that ten rupee note, and anything less feels unsatisfactory. It's as if a part of your routine is missing, leaving you unsettled.

You find it hard to focus in class, your mind consumed by thoughts of what could have been. But here's the question: Are you genuinely dissatisfied, or does this unexpected change in your routine simply throw you off? Think about it. We're all a bit like that kid, aren't we? We form habits and expectations; when they're not met, we often feel let down. But perhaps it's not true dissatisfaction; it might just be our minds playing tricks on us, making us feel upset because things didn't go as planned.

So, the next time you find yourself in a similar situation, take a moment to reflect: Is this really dissatisfaction, or just a temporary hiccup in your expectations? This shift in perspective might just change how you feel. As children, we take these moments very seriously when we don't receive what we expect. However, if we look back on the same scenario with a grown-up mindset, we may realize how insignificant our childhood concerns really were.

Satisfaction is a feeling of contentment and peace within ourselves, regardless of what we have or where we are in life. It's about finding happiness in the present moment, rather than constantly striving for more or worrying about what we lack.

Let me share a story to illustrate this. Once there were two friends named Raghav and Sanjay from Chennai. They planned a month-long tour together, visiting various destinations. Raghav had a charming habit of starting his mornings by wishing the first person he met a good day and treating them to coffee, every day, he makes it a point to thank the universe for even the smallest joys that bring a smile to his face. Through this ritual, he cultivates a sense of contentment, realizing that what he has is truly enough to fill his heart with satisfaction. That doesn't mean he neglects his future aspirations; it simply means he never finds himself in a place where he questions the quality of his life. He's genuinely content with his accomplishments, finding ample reasons to express gratitude to the universe every day for the beauty of his existence and the opportunity of each new day. He was known for his kindness and warm-hearted nature.

On the other hand, Sanjay was more reserved and often preoccupied with worries about his business and other responsibilities, He's never happy because he's always thinking about what's coming next instead of enjoying the current scenario. Wanting more isn't bad, but it's not good when we only focus on the future and ignore the present. He never expressed gratitude for anything because his mind was never content with what he received or what he had already accomplished in life. Even during their time at an ashram, his mind was consumed with thoughts of his properties and business affairs.

One day, Sanjay received troubling news from his business manager: they had lost a major deal. After hearing this, his stress and tension reached a breaking point, causing him to behave rudely towards everyone around him. He attributed his behavior to the many worries weighing on his mind. Suddenly, he collapsed and lost consciousness. Concerned residents of the ashram quickly rushed him to the hospital, where doctors diagnosed him with a stress-induced mental breakdown. It became clear that Sanjay had allowed his worries to overwhelm him, leading to a serious physical illness.

Sanjay's condition shed light on a common phenomenon: the relentless pursuit of wanting more, whether it be wealth, recognition, or success, often leaves individuals feeling perpetually dissatisfied. The story illustrates how stress can manifest when people prioritize their desires over their actual needs, constantly striving for more without finding contentment in the present moment.

Satisfaction, however, doesn't imply complacency or a lack of ambition. Rather, it entails finding peace and happiness in one's current circumstances while still striving for personal growth and improvement. It's about striking a balance between aspirations and appreciation for what one already has.

Reflecting on childhood innocence, where simple joys brought immense happiness, highlights the stark contrast between then and now. As children, even a small treat like a bar of 10-rupee chocolate would light up our faces with joy. However, as adults, we often find ourselves chasing after bigger dreams and aspirations, losing sight of the simple pleasures that once brought us contentment.

It's important to learn how to distinguish between our needs and our desires. Constantly pursuing new goals without acknowledging our current achievements and the things we should be grateful for can create a cycle of never-ending dissatisfaction. Instead, we should focus on cultivating a mindset of gratitude and appreciating the blessings in our lives. Making this shift in perspective can lead to greater peace and happiness, freeing us from the burden of endless desires and stress.

The cycle of constant dissatisfaction can lead many individuals toward depression, as they often stress over unmet desires and uncertainties about the future. It's crucial, therefore, to develop a mindset that values the present moment, appreciates life's simple joys, and understands that true satisfaction comes from within, rather than from external possessions or achievements.

In our busy lives, we often end up pursuing things we don't have instead of appreciating what we're having. Taking a moment each day to practice gratitude can significantly improve our mood and outlook. Gratitude involves noticing and being thankful for the good things in our lives, both big and small.

One easy way to start practicing gratitude is by spending a few moments every day to think about what you're thankful for. You can do this when you wake up, before you go to bed, or whenever you have a quiet moment. Just take a deep breath, center yourself, and think about the things that bring you joy.

It's worth mentioning that gratitude isn't just about the big, exciting moments in life. It's also about appreciating the little things that happen every day. Whether it's a friendly smile, a delicious meal, or a cozy moment with a loved one, there's always something to be grateful for.

If you want to enhance your gratitude practice, consider starting a gratitude journal. At the end of each day, write down three things that you are thankful for. These can range from a kind gesture from a friend to a beautiful sunset you experienced. Writing them down helps to reinforce the feeling of gratitude and serves as a reminder of the positive aspects of your life.

As you continue to practice it, you'll start to notice a shift in how you see the world. Instead of focusing on what you lack, you'll begin to see the abundance of blessings all around you. This shift in perspective can lead to a greater sense of contentment and happiness in your life.

In our generation, we often compare ourselves to others, and when we perceive someone else as being better off, it can lead to dissatisfaction with our own achievements. Take social media, for example. People typically share only their happy moments, which can create the impression that their lives are perfect. When we see this, we might wish our lives were the same and feel as though we're missing out.

There are two ways to respond to this: one is to feel inspired by others' success and learn from it, which is a positive reaction. However, if we start comparing ourselves negatively, it can result in feelings of unhappiness and dissatisfaction. It's essential to remember that what we see online isn't always the complete picture. Focusing on our own journey, rather than comparing ourselves to others, can lead to a more satisfying and fulfilling life.

Here are 5 to-do lists for those who truly desire to feel true satisfaction in life:

1. Start a Daily Gratitude Practice:
- Spend a few minutes in a day to think about your blessings.
- Conserve some time to relish both the grand and minute gifts life hands out.
- Consider keeping a gratitude journal to track your thoughts and feelings.

2. Embrace Present Moments:
- Mindfulness keeps you in the "here and now," where you take note of all those little delights and occurrences throughout your day.
- Don't worry about what lies ahead, and try not to lose sleep over past regrets.

3. Reflect on Needs vs. Desires:
- Take inventory of your wants and distinguish them from your genuine needs.
- Prioritize fulfilling your needs while being mindful of excessive desires.
- Cultivate contentment with what you have rather than constantly seeking more.

4. Seek Balance in Pursuits:
- Strive for personal growth and improvement, but not at the expense of your well-being.
- Set realistic goals that align with your values and bring genuine fulfillment.
- Remember that true satisfaction comes from finding peace and happiness in your current circumstances.

5. <u>Practice Self-Compassion</u>:

- Be kind to yourself and acknowledge that it's okay to feel dissatisfied at times.
- Avoid self-judgment and comparison with others.
- Train yourself to self-acceptance and gratitude for your journey.

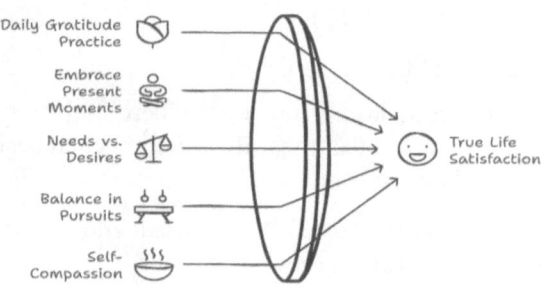

LESSON: - *True satisfaction arises from gratitude, mindfulness, and balance. By valuing the present, distinguishing needs from desires, and fostering self-compassion, we nurture contentment.*

Chapter - 19
Meditation and Mindset

POV: - Welcome to explore the topic of "Meditation and Mindset," a space where we can explore the incredible benefits of meditation for our mental health and emotional well-being. You may have heard that meditation can powerfully impact our minds, but you might be curious about how it truly works. What specific effects does it have on our thoughts, emotions, and stress levels? Together, we will explore the awakening journey of discovery, examining various ways meditation can enhance focus, and promote calmness with a positive mindset.

Have you ever tried meditation? It's a bit like sharpening a blunt knife. Just as a sharp knife glides easily through vegetables, a calm and focused mind can help you see through confusion and negativity. This means you can think more clearly and respond better to life's challenges. Both sharpening a knife and practicing meditation take time and dedication, but the benefits can make a big difference in how you handle everyday situations.

Imagine your mind is like a bustling marketplace, filled with thoughts buzzing around like busy shoppers. Sometimes, these thoughts can become overwhelming, especially when life throws unexpected challenges our way – be it studies, work, relationships, or family responsibilities. It's like carrying a heavy burden that weighs us down.

In today's busy world, we all have responsibilities, whether we enjoy them or not. If you've ever felt this way, you know that unexpected events can come up and cause stress, disrupting our peace of mind. In these moments, it's easy for our thoughts to start racing and feel out of control, which can be really overwhelming. We might find ourselves overthinking things, making it hard to make decisions and handle the challenges we face.

Let me share a story with you. One day, while I was strolling in a park, I noticed an old man observing a stranger sitting on a bench. The stranger appeared very sad, with his hands on his head. I happened to be nearby, so I stood behind them to see what would unfold. After a minute, the old man sat on the same bench and, looking at the stranger, asked if something was bothering him and if he wanted to talk about it.

The sad person turned his head toward the old man to see who was asking him. At first, he responded, "Who are you? Forget it, you can't help me." But the old man replied, "How can I help you if you don't tell me what's bothering you?" I'm just like your father, you can share it with me. The old man's voice felt familiar and concerned to him. Believing in his sincerity, he began to share his story. He explained that he used to run a business with his partner, who was his only childhood friend. Unfortunately, his partner had passed away in an accident not long ago, leaving him all alone. Since they were like brothers, he couldn't forget him. His mind struggled to accept that his friend was gone. This sadness made him feel helpless and even affected his relationships with his family.

Feeling the stranger's pain, the old man asked, "Do you think you can move on from this?" The stranger replied, "I want to, but he was my only friend. We spent every moment together." The old man understood the stranger's struggle and asked if he could suggest something.

The stranger responded positively and hugged the old man, saying it felt good to let out my feelings. I don't know why I didn't talk to anyone before." The old man reassured him, saying, "It's okay."

Now, listen carefully to what I'm going to tell you. When our minds are filled with countless thoughts, we start feeling overwhelmed. That's when we need to find calmness. Whenever I felt the same way, I created a peaceful environment for myself and practiced meditation. This helps me understand why I sometimes feel overwhelmed.

When you meditate, you enter a state where nothing can disturb you—it's just you and your thoughts. At first, the stranger became confused, questioning the impact of meditation. However, as he felt more comfortable, he asked the old man, "What's the best way for me to find help through meditation?"

The old man replied that there are many types of meditation. In your case, he suggested finding a peaceful place and thinking about the good times you shared with your friend. Then, he encouraged him to reflect on the people who are currently in his life, whether they are family or friends.

Thinking back on the happy times you shared with your friend can really brighten your day! It's such a warm feeling to know that you had someone special in your life with whom you made so many wonderful memories. At the same time, it's good to reflect on both the joyful and tough moments you've experienced.

Consider how long those moments lasted—were they just fleeting or did they stick around for a while? You might start to see that nothing in life is permanent. Those tough times won't last forever, and neither will the amazing moments. As the saying goes, "Wo kehte hai na ye samay bhi guzar jayega," or "This too shall pass." It's such an important reminder about the flow of life!

Finding yourself in a peaceful place while trying to calm your mind can truly transform your life. This is one of the most valuable lessons you can learn, which begins with observing your thoughts, feelings, and experiences.

Initiating meditation into our routine allows us to see reality more clearly, calm our minds, and strengthen our inner selves.

I fondly remember my experience at a meditation center called "Vipassana," which is globally recognized for its effectiveness and benefits. This place teaches insightful techniques to better understand life, originally developed by Gautam Buddha. I decided to take a course at Dhamma Ganga Ghat in Kolkata when I was feeling quite desperate. I had been struggling with insomnia for almost a year, and the anxiety that accompanied it had left me feeling completely drained, but when I felt a bit better, I enrolled in a 10-day course there.

The experience was new and a bit overwhelming, especially with the thought of another sleepless night ahead of me. I wanted to escape the constant cycle of fear and tiredness. That's why I decided to sign up for a 10-day Vipassana meditation course. There are many meditation programs out there, but Vipassana felt like the right choice for me. It focuses on finding calm, practicing discipline, and putting in hard work—values that I really connect with. I'm not interested in the more mystical side of meditation, so big groups of overly enthusiastic people don't really appeal to me. I liked how straightforward Vipassana is in its approach.

Vipassana differs from other types of meditation. Instead of just being aware of the moment or repeating a mantra, it's about not reacting to discomfort. Although I had to sit for a longer duration, even when sitting became challenging and my body felt restless, I had to focus on the sensations I experienced. After 10 days of practice, I learned to maintain my calm regardless of what life throws at me. Although Vipassana has roots in Buddhism, the course is completely non-religious. The late Sir S.N. Goenka, who grew up in Myanmar, is recognized as the founder of these retreats. He learned Vipassana meditation in Myanmar and found it to be truly beneficial. Motivated by this experience, he decided to expand its practice for the benefit of society.

When I was planning to attend a Vipassana course, many people questioned why I wanted to put myself through such strict conditions, where I would be unable to talk, make eye contact, or interact with others for a full 10 days, except for asking the teacher any questions I had. I explained that my goal was to gain a deeper understanding of myself and to help my mind prepare for my plans.

Upon arrival, I handed over all my belongings for the next 10 days, and the staff assigned me a room. On the first day, a bell rang outside my door at 4 am, signaling it was time to wake up, even though it was still dark. I rolled out of bed and prepared for the 4:30 am meditation session, which focused on paying attention to our breath. Whenever our minds wandered, we simply had to bring our attention back to our breathing. It seemed so simple yet somewhat pointless at first.

As I followed the instructions, I concentrated on feeling my breath going in and out through my nose. Initially, it felt unimportant, but when the instructor explained its significance, I was amazed by how much Vipassana meditation began to change my daily life. The instructor emphasized that by concentrating on our breath, even when other thoughts arise, we develop the ability to stay focused in challenging situations. This helps our minds become more disciplined and capable of concentrating on what truly matters. This technique is called "ANAPANA" meditation. Vipassana meditation stands apart from other practices like mindfulness meditation, which emphasizes heightened awareness, and transcendental meditation, which relies on a repeated mantra.

Participating in a Vipassana retreat felt just like running a marathon for us. It challenged our minds and bodies to grasp the reality of impermanence—that nothing lasts forever. Whether we're experiencing joy or sadness, pleasure or pain, everything is fleeting. Experiencing this impermanence firsthand during the meditation camp helped us understand why Vipassana is so highly regarded and rejuvenating. It offers a unique perspective on reality, allowing us to truly see and feel the world as it is. In my opinion, every person should experience a 10-day Vipassana retreat at least once in their lifetime for a profound and transformative experience.

Throughout the time, we practiced various meditation techniques and followed our routines. We learned the essence of Vipassana: "Sab Anitya Hai" - everything is impermanent. This realization has proven to be immensely helpful for me.

Imagine spending 10 days in a meditation session. For the first 3 days, you focus solely on your breath. Then, for the next 7 days, you expand your attention to encompass your entire body along with your breath.

During this practice, you begin to notice something profound: all the feelings you experience—whether pleasure, joy, or pain—are temporary. They arise and fade away, just like everything else in life.

This understanding helps me see reality more clearly, much like the lessons taught by Gautama Buddha in Vipassana meditation. The late Sir SN Goenka also played a significant role in spreading this wisdom to people everywhere.

No matter your age or what you are doing, you can begin practicing mindfulness to keep your mind focused. Just as the old man in the park helped a stranger through grief, meditation offers a way to achieve inner peace and resilience in the face of life's challenges. By cultivating mindfulness and acceptance, we can navigate the busy marketplace of our thoughts with grace and tranquility.

I've been trying to explain how valuable meditation can be. Imagine it like going to the gym for your mind—you can't just go once and expect to feel great right away. Just like how your body gets stronger and more fit with regular exercise, the good effects of meditation grow deeper the more you practice it.

While I won't specify any particular techniques, as you can easily find plenty of information online or on YouTube, I want to emphasize an important point: if you truly want to experience the essence of meditation, make sure to attend a 10-day Vipassana meditation camp at least once in your life. The camp is free of charge, and on the last day, you have the option to donate if you wish. You will never regret attending this experience.

Here are some practical tasks for those who wish to benefit from the lessons of this chapter:

1. Incorporate a 10-minute meditation into your daily routine and observe the impact it has on your life.
2. Start keeping a journal to track your emotions and experiences, recognizing their temporary nature.

Practice mindfulness in your daily life by being present in everything you do. Stay focused and pay attention while doing different activities. Take time to observe your surroundings.

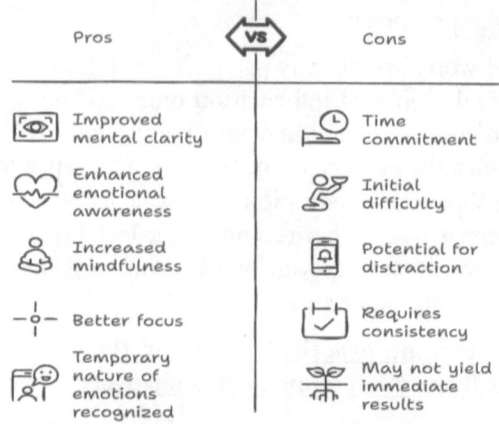

LESSON:- We need to be fit in two ways: mentally and physically. Through consistent workouts and a healthy diet, we can develop good stamina and achieve our desired body shape. Similarly, by practicing meditation regularly, we can enhance our awareness and mindfulness in life.

Chapter - 20
Addictions and their impacts

POV: - Do you understand why we sometimes become addicted to certain things? Have you ever found yourself in a phase where you're trying to break free from a habit or routine that has turned into an addiction? This often occurs when we feel lonely or have too much idle time. Something that initially brought us pleasure can become a regular part of our lives, eventually transforming into an addiction. Today, we will not only learn about the consequences of addiction and its effects but also gain a deeper understanding of how to overcome it. We will explore why people often get so caught up in their addictions.

I think calling certain behaviors "addictions" might not tell the whole story. To me, it feels more like a way we bond with things that bring us joy and pleasure. These could be activities or substances that make us feel fulfilled and become part of our daily lives. However, sometimes when we get caught up in these things, we might not notice that they can leave us feeling a bit empty inside. That emptiness can make it harder to make the choices we want and live our lives to the fullest.

The way we connect with the things around us really shapes our future! Our environment, the people we spend time with, and our surroundings all play a big role in influencing us. The relationships we build and the activities we engage in are all connected to this.

It's easy to develop habits around things like binge-watching movies, indulging in junk food, enjoying a drink, getting lost in digital games, scrolling through reels, smoking, or watching adult content. We often dive into these activities without even realizing how they affect our lives. It's completely normal to have cravings, but when we find ourselves wanting these things over and over, they can turn into habits we're not always happy with.

While these activities can be fun and bring us joy, it's important to recognize that they can also lead to some not-so-great consequences. Everything we do has its own outcomes, so improving our decision-making skills over time can really make a difference! As we learn and grow, we become better at making choices. Just remember that every little decision leads to some results—then why not aim for the choices that bring us the best outcomes?

Let me share a little story with you. Meet Aakash, a cheerful young boy who was living in Mumbai with his parents. His life was quite normal until one day when his father received a transfer letter that took the whole family to a new city Chennai. It was a big change for Aakash, who had to leave behind the familiar sights and sounds he loved.

At home, things were a bit challenging because his parents were dealing with their own issues, which made the atmosphere feel a little tense, creating a bit of toxicity. With no friends in Chennai, Aakash felt increasingly isolated.

One evening, Aakash saw his dad and a friend sitting together, enjoying some chilled beer and having some gossip. His dad's friend, who doesn't drink, asked, "Why do you drink so much every day?" Aakash's dad replied very calmly, "SUKOON HAI, APNE DARD KI DAWA HAI YE." Aakash had always seen his dad drinking alcohol to cope with his stress and then falling asleep. Aakash thought maybe alcohol could help him feel better too. As he couldn't drink at home, he planned to sneak into a bar and start hanging out. There, he found temporary relief in the company of strangers who shared his newfound habit.

As days turned into weeks, weeks into months, Aakash's visits to the bar became a routine. He found a new group of people there and started enjoying the company, but he didn't realize he was getting addicted to that environment which was destroying him from the inside.

He stopped caring about his school tasks, his chores, and even himself.

By the time his parents noticed a change in his behavior but it was too late. Aakash has gone deep with his addiction. So, what do you think? what led him to this point? Was it the fighting between his parents at home? The loneliness? The influence of new friends? Or maybe his parents not paying attention to him?

In truth, it was a combination of all these factors that lured Aakash into a world of addiction.

Each experience made it more difficult for him to think clearly and caused him to act in ways he never imagined he would. Now, Aakash is facing the consequences of his actions, and his ability to make sound decisions is not as clear as it once was.

As we observe, "We notice that Aakash feels better and less lonely when he's doing something, but he doesn't realize it's only a short-term fix. In the long run, his addictions are actually making his life harder and hurting him inside."

Many young people today are facing addiction issues, and we might wonder about the reason. Is it because they are associating with the wrong crowd, living in toxic environments, or perhaps they just lack an understanding of life?

It seems that a lot of parents and teachers really focus on academic success, which is important for sure! But are we sometimes forgetting to teach our youth about life itself? Things like the risks of addiction or the value of self-awareness can be just as crucial.

If we take a moment to look around, we might notice that not many people have had the chance to learn about these essential life skills. Many prioritize academics, often calling it "bookish knowledge" or "KITABI GYAN." While that foundation is valuable, it doesn't completely prepare us for the ups and downs that life throws our way. Let's discuss how we can create a more balanced approach to education that includes these important lessons!

Consider this: if someone doesn't excel in traditional subjects like math or science doesn't mean they aren't talented or full of potential! There are amazing singers who don't need to know algebra, athletes who value their physical fitness more than physics, and fantastic writers who don't rely on chemistry. Everyone has their own unique skills and strengths—it's all about embracing and developing them instead of feeling pressured to fit into a rigid mold.

When we celebrate and nurture these individual talents, it can help steer us away from addictive behaviors. These passions are the key that sometimes guides us toward positive choices and keeps us moving in a healthy direction!

Fundamentally, there are a few important aspects of life that really shape the choices we make and how we act. That's why, in addition to the academic lessons, it's so important for parents, teachers, and schools to share insights about real-life situations too. This means discussing and being open to talk about topics like addiction, critical thinking, behavior, sex education, and other real-world issues that we are also exploring in different parts of this book.

Only by addressing these topics, we can truly educate individuals about humanity, society, and proper behavior. It's about providing a well-rounded education that prepares youth for the complexities of the world they live in.

There's no magical solution, like a "BRAMHASTRA," that will make your problems vanish forever. However, you can achieve genuine realizations by following the methods I'm about to share. I will guide you through practical steps and help you regularly ask yourself important questions as part of a routine until you feel liberated from the mental struggles of addiction.

How about taking a little moment today to pause and think about your life and what's around you? In those quiet moments, we might spot some sneaky patterns of habits that we didn't even realize were creeping in. It could be something like scrolling through social media for hours or grabbing that third cup of coffee when you know it's time to stop. It's all about being mindful and noticing those little things!

<u>When you notice yourself slipping into an unfavorable kind of behavior, it's a great time to pause and ask yourself some questions:</u>

1. Is this habit actually not harmful to you? Think about how it's impacting your life.
2. Are you missing out on important moments, and feeling drained because of it?
3. And here's a big one: what will happen if you continue this behavior?
4. Can you imagine living with this habit for the rest of your life?

After reflecting on these questions, it's time to focus on potential solutions.

1. Is there a way out?
2. Can you break free from this behavioral cycle?
3. Think about all possible options for change.
4. Begin brainstorming and visualize how your life could transform if you embraced one of these solutions.
5. Would it be better? More fulfilling?

<u>Now, here's the real kicker:</u>

Do you really need to kick this habit? You might be surprised by the answer! If you're ready to take that exciting leap and put in some effort, then here's a little promise to make to yourself: celebrate every single step you take! Treat yourself to each little win along the way to becoming a healthier and happier version of yourself. You've got this!

Lastly, just keep in mind that Self-reflection is like tuning a musical instrument. Just as a musician takes the time to adjust the strings to ensure they are in harmony, we need to pause and check in on our behaviors and thoughts to make sure they resonate positively in our lives. If we ignore those adjustments, the music of our life can easily fall out of tune, leading to annoyance rather than harmony.

I hope you realize how significantly this mental illness affects your life.

Below are five to-do lists, and I genuinely hope you approach them with sincere intent.

1. <u>Self-Reflection:</u> Take a moment each day to reflect on your life. If you notice any patterns of addictive behavior, think about how they impact your well-being.

2. <u>Questioning Habits</u>: Challenge yourself to question your habits regularly. Look upon if your habits are truly helpful. Consider how they affect your daily life and what might happen if you keep them up.

3. <u>Exploring Solutions</u>: When you identify a habit or behavior that you want to change, explore potential solutions.

4. <u>Seeking Support</u>: Don't hesitate to reach out for support if you're struggling with addictive behaviors. Whether it's talking to friends, and family, or seeking professional help—remember you're not alone.

5. <u>Celebrating Progress</u>: Celebrate every step forward on your journey. Acknowledge and reward yourself for all your victories, big and small!

LESSON: *- Always keep in mind that your life and its goals surpass any addictive behavior you seek for momentary dopamine pleasure in your mind.*

Chapter - 21
Follow the phenomena we learn

POV: - "FOLLOW THE PHENOMENA WE LEARN" Yes, you heard it right. You may be wondering why I dedicated a chapter to this topic. It's crucial. When we reflect on ourselves, we realize that 90% of what we hear, read, or learn often fades away as a one-time understanding. We tend to forget or become lazy when it comes to implementing these insights into our lives. Even after reading this book, only a few will truly apply the knowledge and lessons gained. Therefore, it's crucial to explore how we absorb and overlook things that could enhance the value of our lives.

Let's start by thinking about whether adapting to new things we learn is important to us. If it doesn't feel relevant, it's okay to skip it here! However, it's helpful to recognize the benefits of being adaptable. It can lead to us becoming better individuals and help us apply new, positive things we learn in our lives.

There's a saying, "Knowing stuff is pointless unless we put it to use." And isn't it funny how often we overlook useful things or just don't feel like acting on them? This seems especially true these days with young people, like those in Gen Z, who can easily spend hours scrolling through social media but might shy away from watching a quick video that could actually teach them something valuable. It really makes you wonder: Why do we tend to ignore opportunities that could make a big difference in our lives and choose to do nothing instead?

Before we can start doing anything, we have to figure out what really matters to us. Then, once we've listened carefully and understood, we can actually start doing stuff. Every day, we come across loads of things, but not everything is useful or important. But when we find something that seems like it could make a difference in our lives, we should take note of it right away.

I'm not telling you anything new, you already know everything. But I'm here to remind you to pay attention to what's important and what's not. It's like a waking-up call to the fact that you need to recognize what matters to you and what does not.

In today's world, there are countless sources of information and many different kinds of knowledge available to us. However, having access to too much information can actually be harmful. We can't learn everything, so we should focus on the information that will be most useful to us right now. For example, if someone is studying to become a doctor (MBBS) but also tries to explore different courses or subject materials at the same time, they might end up confused and not very good at anything. It's great to have knowledge in different areas, but everything has its time. We should focus on a limited amount of information that we know is valuable to us and that we can use in our lives. It's better to have a little information that we can actually use than a lot of information that we can't do anything with.

Why Implementation Matters

"Learning is only beneficial if we can apply what we learn." When we use new knowledge in real life, we gain a deeper understanding, develop new skills, and experience personal and professional growth. Without practical application, we are likely to forget what we've learned. This idea can be illustrated through the experiences of two individuals, Rohan and Alok, who both seek valuable information but approach it in very different ways.

Let me explain this through their story.

The Employee of the Year

In a well-known city in India, Mumbai, where people constantly rush to get ahead of one another, there were two colleagues, Rohan and Alok, who worked side by side in the marketing department of a fast-growing tech company. Both were recognized for their enthusiasm for learning and their dedication to their jobs. However, their approaches to handling information were quite different.

Rohan: The Knowledge Collector

Rohan was a person who always tried to impress his colleagues with a wealth of information. He spent hours each day reading articles, attending webinars, and taking online courses. His desk was often cluttered with notebooks filled with ideas and strategies. He loved discussing the latest trends in marketing and technology with his colleagues, consistently impressing them with his extensive knowledge. However, Rohan frequently moved on to new topics without applying what he had learned.

His morning routine involved skimming through news feeds and checking his email. He read about the latest productivity hacks but rarely implemented them. His mornings were often rushed, and he frequently arrived at work just in time, if not late.

At work, Rohan was known for his innovative ideas, but his projects often lagged behind schedule. He juggled multiple tasks, switching between them as new information caught his interest. Despite his vast knowledge, his output was inconsistent, and his projects often missed deadlines. At the same time, he worked alongside his colleague, Alok.

Alok: The Practical Learner

Alok, like Rohan, had a passion for learning. However, Alok focused on limited information that he knew he could apply directly to his work and life. He carefully selected what he learned and made sure to put it into practice.

Alok's mornings were well-organized. He started with a review of his daily goals, followed by exercise and a healthy breakfast. He read a chapter from a book on personal development and took notes on actionable insights. Alok implemented these insights into his daily routine, steadily building effective habits.

As a project manager in the same department, Alok used project management techniques he had learned to organize his tasks and team efficiently. He applied new strategies step by step, ensuring they were effective before moving on to other concepts. Alok's projects were delivered on time, and his team appreciated his practical approach. His desk was neat and focused on current tasks rather than future possibilities. His focus on implementation allowed him to see tangible results from his efforts, leading to a satisfying sense of accomplishment.

Both were working harder as the season of the "Employee of the Year award" going to be announced soon.

In December, the end of the year, the company held its annual Employee of the Year award ceremony. Everyone in the department was excited, and the air was filled with anticipation. Rohan confirmed in his mind that the reward will surely get to him only until he hear the announcement from the CEO that the employee of the year award goes to Alok. Now, he is the winner, the room erupted in applause. Alok's consistent performance, ability to implement new strategies, and dedication to his work had paid off. He became very happy, everyone was congratulating him one by one.

Rohan, on the other hand, was surprised and disappointed. He took a drink and went into a corner, looking very sad. His boss noticed his unhappy expression and wanted to cheer him up. Rohan felt it was unfair that he didn't win the award, and he was eager to find out why. When his boss asked him why he looked so sad, Rohan didn't hold back and asked the question that was bothering him.

"Sir, can I ask you something?" Rohan began hesitantly.

"Of course, Rohan. What's on your mind?" The Boss replied.

"Just curious, actually, why didn't I win this Employee of the Year award?"

I've worked hard and learned so much this year," Rohan said, his voice tinged with frustration.

The Boss smiled kindly. "Rohan, there's no doubt that you are very knowledgeable and hardworking. But knowledge alone isn't enough. What sets Alok apart is his ability to implement what he learns. He applies new strategies and techniques effectively in his work. That's why his projects are always on time and meet the company's goals."

Rohan looked thoughtful. "So, you're saying that it's not just about how much I know, but how I use that knowledge?"

"Exactly," His Boss replied. "Learning has value, but what makes a difference is the application of what you've learned."

Alok focuses on a smaller amount of information, but he makes sure to apply it in his daily work. That's what makes him successful."

A Lesson Learned:

Rohan left the office deep in thought. He realized that while he had gathered a lot of information, he hadn't taken the time to implement any of it. Inspired by Alok's success, Rohan decided to change his approach. He would focus on practical application instead of just accumulating knowledge.

From that day forward, Rohan began to prioritize implementation in his work. He set clear goals and applied new strategies, which led to gradual improvements in his performance. While he still loved learning, he focused on using the knowledge he gained effectively, rather than simply accumulating information to impress his colleagues.

Conclusion: Embrace Practical Application of Knowledge

Rohan and Alok's story illustrates the significance of not only acquiring knowledge but also applying it effectively. Although Rohan possessed extensive knowledge, his failure to put it into practice kept him at a disadvantage compared to Alok. Alok's ability to apply what he learned enabled him to excel and ultimately win the Employee of the Year award. This story emphasizes that the true value of learning lies in its application. It's important to "embrace the phenomena we learn" and implement them, rather than simply accumulating information without utilizing it.

It's crucial to recognize that the real importance lies not in gathering vast amounts of information, but in having a limited set of useful knowledge that you can apply in real life.

Here are some practical tasks you can incorporate into your life that will have a positive impact if you choose to implement them.

1. <u>Set Clear, Actionable Goals</u>: After reading this chapter, sit on your bed or chair and reflect on where your interests lie and what areas are growing for you. Then, set that as your goal for a specific timeframe.

2. <u>Apply What You Learn</u>: - Now, after identifying your defined goal, think about the knowledge that is relevant to your goal that you've learned, and implement it ASAP!

3. <u>Reflect and Review Regularly</u>: - Reflect daily on what you've learned and applied. Conduct weekly reviews of your progress and learn from mistakes to refine your approach.

Implementing Knowledge for Personal Growth

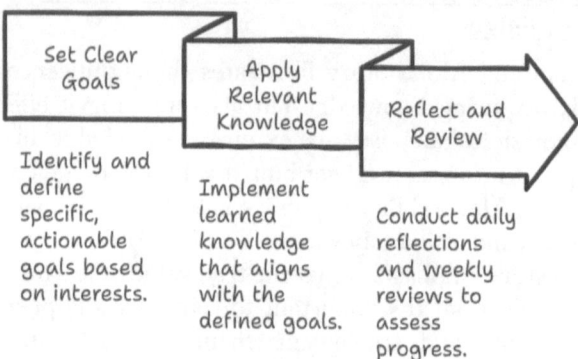

Set Clear Goals
Identify and define specific, actionable goals based on interests.

Apply Relevant Knowledge
Implement learned knowledge that aligns with the defined goals.

Reflect and Review
Conduct daily reflections and weekly reviews to assess progress.

<u>**LESSON:**</u> - *Knowledge gains true significance when we prioritize applying what we learn. It's not merely about acquiring information; it's about harnessing it effectively in our lives.*

Chapter - 22
Quality determine results

POV: - In this chapter, we will explore the importance of qualitative aspects in our lives. We will examine how adopting a qualitative approach sets us apart from those who only focus on casually getting things done. We will delve into the principle that "Quality Determines Results." Discover how prioritizing quality over quantity can lead to more meaningful outcomes in various areas of life.

Here, we'll explore how the principles we learned in the previous chapter, "Follow the Phenomena We Learn," relate to the importance of quality in our actions.

Just as we've discussed the value of implementing what we learn, it's essential to recognize that the quality of our approach greatly influences the outcomes we achieve. In today's fast-paced world, where competition is fierce, we're often presented with choices: to prioritize quantity or to prioritize quality. Think about this: Imagine your friend is studying hard for 4 hours each day. He puts his phone away and avoids distractions completely. Now, on the other hand, you're studying for 8 hours, but you're taking breaks and chatting with friends in between. When your parents see you both, they might think you're the really dedicated one because you're at it for longer. But honestly, who do you think will end up learning more? Your friend, with those focused 4 hours, or you with your 8 hours filled with distractions? It's an interesting thing to consider when it comes to getting the most out of your study time!

Reflecting on our daily experiences, we recognize that every action we take, whether it's exercising, studying, working, or making decisions, holds significance. It's not just about going through the motions; it's about doing things well. And this is where the connection lies: when we follow the aspects we've learned and prioritize quality, our actions become more purposeful.

Think of the analogy of going to the gym: Imagine a beginner who goes to the gym twice a day but ignores the trainer's advice and does their own thing. Now compare that to someone who only works out for one hour but diligently follows the trainer's instructions and maintains a healthy lifestyle. It's evident who will achieve better results. Similarly, in both our personal and professional lives, prioritizing quality over quantity leads to more meaningful outcomes.

But why does quality matter? Because it's about more than just completing tasks; it's about doing them well. It's about investing the time and effort to ensure that our actions are aligned with our goals and values. By prioritizing quality, we not only achieve better results but also cultivate a sense of satisfaction in our endeavors.

Think of quality in your actions like baking a cake. You can rush the process and toss in a handful of ingredients without measuring, excited to see a finished product quickly. However, if you take your time to carefully measure each ingredient, mix them properly, and follow the recipe, you'll end up with a delicious cake that everyone enjoys. Just like in baking, when we prioritize quality over quantity in our actions, we create results that are not just acceptable but truly satisfying and fulfilling.

So, as we continue our journey of growth and learning, let's remember the importance of quality in everything we do. By following the aspects we've learned and prioritizing quality in our actions, we set ourselves up for success and fulfillment. Quality truly does determine results, and by embracing this principle, we can navigate life's challenges with confidence and purpose.

<u>For this chapter, I won't list multiple tasks like before. Instead, I'll suggest one single action to take after reading:</u>

<u>Your task is straightforward</u>: Sit down with a notebook and make a list of the things in life that you feel you haven't done well. For each thing you've noted, write three reasons why you think you didn't succeed. This exercise will help you identify areas where you may need to focus on improving your overall approach to life.

<u>LESSON</u>:- Quantity reflects your commitment, while quality demonstrates your exceptional standards.

Chapter - 23
The change and its consequences

POV: - *We've covered a significant aspect that we must know and acknowledge in life. Change is a universal truth that no one is unfamiliar with; The key difference lies in whether we pursue positive or negative change. This ultimately depends on our actions, as <u>"Taking no action is also an action that determines changes in time"</u>. If you've really followed the things mentioned, you've surely seen some changes in your personality. In this chapter, we'll be talking about this only: how things change and what consequences we have to bear.*

This chapter presents a key concept that defines how our perspectives and the changes we experience in our lives are influenced by our actions.

Let me simplify this idea for you. What are your thoughts on change? Can change be beneficial?

The answer can vary based on different factors and actions. When we consider the practicality of change, we often find that when we attempt to make significant changes in pursuit of a goal, we frequently encounter failure, leading to feelings of demotivation, stress, and anxiety. Why does this happen? Is it because we lack consistency, discipline, or dedication to improving our lives? I don't believe so.

The main reason we struggle to transform is our expectation of immediate results, which can be very challenging. However, what if we focused on making small changes, improving by just 1% each day? While these improvements might not be noticeable at first, consistent effort over time can lead to significant progress. By adopting this approach, minor changes accumulate and enhance our overall abilities in a greater way.

This principle also applies when we procrastinate and avoid making changes, believing we can start tomorrow. The negative effects of small, continuous inaction can accumulate over time. If you procrastinate every day and keep deferring your goals, you'll never achieve them. As the saying goes, "Kal na Kisi ka aaya hai na Kisi ka Aayega" (Tomorrow never comes for anyone). It's essential to grasp this concept very clearly.

If you are familiar with mutual funds, you understand how compounding works over time. Just as our investments grow through regular contributions and compounding, our actions also multiply as we repeat them. For example, going to the gym four days a week might not yield immediate results. Similarly, saving a little money regularly won't make you a millionaire overnight. Studying for an hour today won't make you a master of a subject, and following a good diet plan for a single day won't show instant changes. These small, consistent actions may not seem significant at first, and we often revert to our previous routines. However, it's important to recognize that, in the long run, these actions do add up.

On the flip side, eating junk food for just one day isn't likely to harm you significantly. Studying less for an hour won't ruin your life either. However, these small missteps can accumulate over time. When these actions become habits, whether they are good or bad, their impact becomes noticeable in the long term.

"Action Taker" OR "Action Thinker"?

If you think, you can observe that there are two kinds of people around you: the "ACTION TAKER" and the "ACTION THINKER." An action thinker is someone who reads the entire content but hasn't followed a single thing. They simply find the content relevant and feel good reading paragraphs. But an action taker, on the other hand, is someone who has a motive behind everything they do. They follow and try to implement what they've learned. Both will see a change in themselves: the action thinker will see the change in time that has gone without anything productive, while the action taker will see growth in life with small changes. Now, it's up to you to decide who you aspire to become in life: an "Action Thinker" or an "Action Taker"?

It's up to you to decide what changes you want in your life. Once you know the changes you want, you'll need to take specific actions to achieve them. We're all here to make changes and contribute to transformation. Remember, with every action we take, we create real and impactful change.

If we pay attention, we can see that many factors influence the changes we make in our lives. These factors serve as the foundation for our decisions, as we base our choices on the outcomes they create. We have all made mistakes throughout our lives, often for a range of reasons—some of which we may not fully understand. However, it's important to reflect on these mistakes to identify where we went wrong and how we can make better decisions in the future.

Here are some to-do lists that will help define and improve your decision-making and correction skills:

(NOTE: - make 4 columns in your diary)

1. Reflect on Past Mistakes

- Write down the aspects in your life where you think you made wrong decisions.

2. Analyze Your Approach

- Think about the approaches you took that led to those wrong turns in your life.

3. Assess Your Current Behavior

- Observe whether you are still making those mistakes or if you have corrected them.

4. <u>Plan for Improvement</u>
- If you are still repeating the same mistakes, write down what you think is the correct way to deal with them.

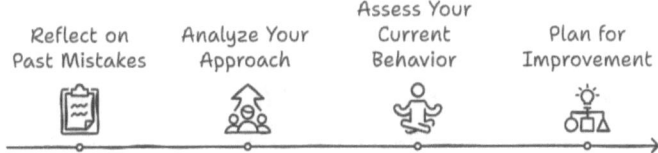

<u>**LESSON**</u>: - *"Embrace change, as it helps us grow and leads to new opportunities in life."*

Chapter - 24
Spiritualism

POV: We are finally here moving into the topic of spiritualism. What do you think about spiritual matters? Is it about worshiping a god or goddess? Is it just about fasting and living on water for a whole day? Or is it something more practical? Often, our perspectives on spiritualism can differ greatly. This isn't just another subject; it has the potential to transform how we live if we learn to incorporate it into our daily lives. Today's youth face numerous challenges. While everyone experiences tough times, people respond to them in different ways. Some complain and make excuses, while others understand that excuses won't bring any change in their lives. Recognizing this difference is crucial! Once you understand these concepts and begin taking action, you can move on your journey into spiritualism.

If you reached this chapter, it means you're genuinely seeking improvement in your life. Congratulations! This shows you have a mindset geared toward learning, which puts you ahead of many others. You've made a valuable choice to pursue personal growth and upgrade yourself on a path of development. Let's move forward with this amazing understanding of spiritualism.

WHAT'S SPIRITUALISM?

I'd love to share some thoughts about spiritualism that might open your mind a bit and show you why it can be so important, especially for teenagers and young adults.

In our fast-paced world, it's interesting to see how many people still hold onto superstitions and often mix them up with spiritualism. It's really important to remember that everyone has their own beliefs and perspectives.

Spiritualism isn't a one-size-fits-all concept; what feels spiritual to one person might be completely different for someone else. It's all about your personal journey and the experiences that shape your viewpoints.

It's also common to confuse spiritualism with religion, but they're not the same thing! You can think of spiritualism as "the spirit behind the rituals." It's all about the level of devotion you put into what you're doing, which helps define your spirituality. The realm of spirituality is incredibly vast—there's so much out there that our minds may not fully understand. But we can start by focusing on its core idea: it's about understanding karma and how it influences the outcomes we experience in life. Embracing these concepts can really deepen your understanding of what spirituality means to you!

Spiritualism for Youngsters

First of all, think about what comes to your mind about spiritualism.

Spirituality can take many forms for youths, helping them connect with their inner self, discover their lifework, and tackle the challenges that life throws their way. It doesn't have to be tied to a specific religion; instead, it's often about being mindful, self-aware, and tapping into something greater than ourselves. Personally, I find my spiritual connection through writing and exploring nature, where I can soak in the sounds of chirping birds and feel the warm sun and gentle touch of mesmerizing air.

Anything that helps you feel reconnected with yourself can be a part of spiritualism.

Imagine it as planting seeds in a garden. Just as a gardener nurtures their plants with water and sunlight, young people can cultivate their spirituality by tending to their inner thoughts and feelings. With time, patience, and care, these seeds can grow into a vibrant garden of self-discovery and connection, bringing beauty, peace, and purpose to their lives.

A STORY TO UNDERSTAND SPIRITUALISM

In a cozy little town, there lived a friend named Jayesh. He was a kind-hearted guy, but lately, he had been feeling a bit lost. After facing the same exam four times and not getting the results he hoped for, his confidence began to waver. School, college, relationships—all of it seemed like a tough uphill battle for him. He felt like a puzzle missing some pieces, and nothing seemed to fit right.

One day, while taking a pleasant walk to clear his head, Jayesh noticed something interesting—a dusty old book left on a bench as if it were waiting for someone to pick it up. He looked around, hoping to see the person who might have forgotten it, but no one showed up. Feeling curious, he decided to take the book home with him. Although it was a bit worn and had a faded cover, he discovered that the pages inside were filled with a touching conversation between a wise monk and a man who was struggling with his worries.

Jayesh felt an instant connection to the story—it was like reading about his own life! The themes of spiritualism, personal growth, and self-discovery spoke to him in a way that brought a sense of comfort.

Determined to find out the owner to return the book, Jayesh began visiting that bench every evening, hoping to see the book's owner. But as time went on, the bench became his special place, and he found himself happily sitting there for hours, reading and soaking up the wisdom. In just four days, he finished the book, but he didn't stop at just reading. He eagerly took notes on the key points that resonated with him and started applying the advice to his life.

To his delight, Jayesh found that the insights from the book were making a real difference. Slowly but surely, the missing pieces of his puzzle started to come together, and he began to feel more hopeful and confident about his journey ahead. With a warm smile on his face, he embraced the exciting transformation that was unfolding in his life.

He noted all the key points that he believed would be beneficial and relevant to his journey. Would you like to know those key points he noted down for himself? Here they are:

1. <u>Self-Reflection</u>

Jayesh decided to start with a simple practice from the book: daily journaling. Each night, he wrote about his thoughts, feelings, and experiences. At first, it was hard to put his emotions into words, but as days went by, he began to understand himself better. Alongside journaling, he practiced mindfulness by spending a few minutes each day in quiet reflection or deep breathing.

2. <u>Positive Actions</u>

Inspired by a book he read, Jayesh began to perform small acts of kindness. He helped many people and volunteered at a local community center. Additionally, he started a gratitude practice, writing down three things he was thankful for each day. These actions not only made him feel good, but they also helped him connect with others in a meaningful way.

3. <u>Setting Goals</u>

Jayesh understood that he needed to set meaningful goals. He began with small, achievable goals like improving his grades and learning a new skill. Every week, he looked at his progress and changed his goals if necessary. Over time, he noticed improvements and felt accomplished.

4. <u>Connection with Others</u>

He made an effort to surround himself with positive influences. He joined a local book club and engaged in conversations with people who inspired him. He found a sense of belonging in a community that shared his interests and values.

5. <u>Learning and Growth</u>

Jayesh was curious about spirituality, so he explored different views. He read books, listened to podcasts, and attended workshops on personal growth and spirituality. This journey helped him find what resonated with him and supported his path.

6. <u>Practicing Meditation</u>

Jayesh noticed that the man in the book struggled with a chaotic mind, and he decided to follow the Monk's advice to practice meditation. At first, concentrating was difficult, but with daily practice, he began to experience a sense of calm. He also started prioritizing his tasks by making a daily list. Over time, Jayesh realized that a significant portion of his thoughts were unnecessary worries that were causing him stress.

7. <u>Balancing Life</u>

Jayesh started to focus on balance in his life by adopting healthy habits. He improved his time management by balancing work, studying, relaxing, and exercising. When stress increased, he used methods like exercising and talking to friends to handle it effectively.[1]

Over the months, Jayesh underwent an incredible transformation, evolving from a lost boy into a vibrant seeker of personal growth and spirituality. His journey was a thrilling mix of highs and lows, each moment bringing him closer to understanding himself and his place in the world. He learned that spirituality isn't about perfection but the exciting quest for improvement and authentic connections with himself and others.

Jayesh's story is an inspiring example of how a simple quest for self-discovery and practical steps can lead to significant personal growth and a more fulfilling life.

---

[1]

Here are five practical "To-Do" tasks inspired by Jayesh's journey and the insights from this chapter on spiritualism:

1. Start a Daily Journaling Practice

- Action: Set aside 10-15 minutes each day to write about your thoughts, feelings, and experiences.

- Purpose: Helps in self-reflection, clarity of thought, and emotional understanding. Track your progress and insights to see how your perspective evolves with time.

2. Perform Acts of Kindness

- Action: Choose one small act of kindness to perform each day, such as helping someone in need, complimenting someone, or volunteering your time.

- Purpose: Builds connections with others and improves your well-being. Regular acts of kindness help create a positive mindset and provide a sense of fulfillment.

3. Set and Review Personal Goals

- Action: Define three specific, achievable goals for the month. Break them into smaller tasks and review your progress weekly.

- Purpose: Provides direction and a sense of accomplishment. Adjusting goals based on your progress keeps you motivated and focused on what truly matters to you.

4. Incorporate Meditation into Your Routine

- Action: Spend 5-10 minutes each day practicing meditation.

- Purpose: Helps in reducing stress, enhancing concentration, and gaining a clearer perspective on your thoughts.

5. <u>Engage in Lifelong Learning</u>
- <u>Action</u>: Set aside a specific time each week to explore new ideas that can help you grow.
- <u>Purpose</u>: Expands your understanding and perspectives, contributing to personal development.

By incorporating these activities into your daily routine, you'll nurture personal growth and strengthen your connection with both yourself and the world around you. Small, consistent actions can lead to meaningful transformation. Stay curious, be patient with yourself, and allow your journey to unfold with intention and sincerity.

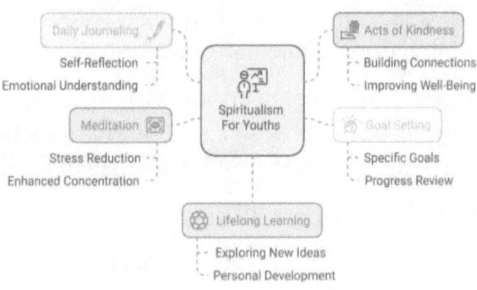

<u>LESSON</u>: - You've reached the end of this book, and that's a fantastic accomplishment! Your dedication to growth is truly special, so congratulations! As you finish this chapter on spiritualism, remember that personal growth starts with self-awareness and intentional actions. By reflecting daily, practicing kindness, setting goals, and being mindful, you're building a meaningful and balanced life. Enjoy your journey ahead! All the Best.

The 4D framework

NOTE: - For a clearer understanding of the 4Ds framework, please refer to the illustration provided at the end.

Embrace the 4Ds Framework: A Guide to Organizing Your Daily Tasks and Goals

For those committed to defining their daily tasks and achieving their goals, the 4D framework is an invaluable tool. This simple yet powerful system helps you classify and prioritize what's truly important. By organizing your tasks into four columns—DO, DON'T, DOING, and DONE—you can streamline your efforts and ensure you're always on track. Here's a detailed look at each component:

DO

Purpose: List tasks and goals that are essential and must be accomplished.

Description: These are your top priorities. They reflect your commitments and the steps needed to achieve your long-term goals. Focus on these tasks to make meaningful progress every day.

DON'T

Purpose: Identify actions and behaviors to avoid.

Description: Recognizing what you shouldn't do is as crucial as knowing what you should be doing. This column helps you eliminate distractions and unproductive habits that can derail your efforts. Stay clear of these pitfalls to maintain your focus and efficiency.

DOING

Purpose: Track what you're currently working on.

Description: This column represents your active tasks. By keeping a real-time record of what you're doing, you can better manage your workload and ensure you're not overcommitting yourself. It also helps in maintaining momentum and avoiding procrastination.

DONE

Purpose: Celebrate your accomplishments.

Description: Once you complete a task, move it to this column. This not only gives you a sense of achievement but also provides a clear record of your progress. Reflecting on what you've done reinforces your efforts and motivates you to keep going.

How to Use the 4Ds Framework

1. <u>Set Up Your Diary</u>: Create four columns labeled as I attached here DO, DON'T, DOING, and DONE.

2. <u>Prioritize Tasks</u>: At the beginning of each day, fill in the DO and DON'T columns based on your goals and priorities.

3. <u>Monitor Progress</u>: As you work through your day, update the DOING column to reflect your active tasks.

4. <u>Reflect and Adjust</u>: At the end of the day, move completed tasks to the DONE column and review your progress. Adjust your plan for the next day accordingly.

4D Framework Task Management

By regularly using the 4Ds framework, you can effectively manage your time, stay focused on your goals, and achieve a balanced and productive life. Embrace this method to transform your daily routine and reach your full potential.

THE FRAMEWORK:

Sl No.	TASKS	DOs	DON'Ts	DOING	DONE

Acknowledgment

As I write this acknowledgment, I wonder if people will genuinely apply the insights I've shared which are drawn from my experiences as a teenager and a young adult. It's evident that the richest 1% of the world's population owns more than 47% of the world's wealth, yet I believe that there are individuals who aspire to be more than just existing; they want to live fully and thrive by embracing the challenges and opportunities that come their way.

If even one person finds value in this book and benefits from it, I will consider my efforts worthwhile.

I won't label my work a masterpiece; instead, I trust that you yourself will recognize its worth based on your own growth, understanding, and personal significance. It has taken me years to reach this final acknowledgment page, and I'm really proud of this journey. The tremendous support I've received, the lessons learned from various mindsets, and the insights gained from today's youth have all contributed to the depth of this work.

I want to take a moment to express my deep gratitude to my parents for their constant motivation, which has been a guiding light throughout my journey in writing this book. I'm equally thankful to my brothers for their unwavering support; A heartfelt thanks to my friends: Ayush Raj, whose companionship has been invaluable; Shashank Jain, who has helped me choose a wonderful title; Arya Kedia, who shared creative insights that shaped the content in initial phases; one of my guide, my teacher; Respected Abhijeet Aich Sir whom I admire to have as one of my valuable support, and Sneha Barnwal, whose presence was instrumental during the time. Your encouragement and support have truly made a difference in this journey.

I also extend a special thank you to the dedicated team at BlueRose. Tejas, Rishabh, Aman, and all others, your dedication and genuine contributions have greatly enriched this book. I am deeply appreciative of all that you have done.

Additionally, I want to take a moment to express my heartfelt gratitude to my friends, whose presence is incredibly important to me. You believed in me and patiently awaited the release of this book. Your unwavering support means so much to me. Thank you to Roshan Barnwal, Jaya Modi, Aakriti Chowdhury, Mukund Kumar, Deepanshu Ranjan, Akansha Barnwal, Kunal Saw, Aayush Pujari, Anish Anand, Ankit Kumar Saw, Supriya Kumari, Aditya, and everyone else with whom I've had meaningful conversations throughout this journey. Your presence in my life has truly made a difference, and I am incredibly grateful to have you by my side. Thank you for everything.

This book is more than simply a collection of words; it's a celebration of the importance of support. While writing it, I've realized that every challenge teaches us something valuable, and every obstacle can lead to a new opportunity. I hope this book connects with you and brings you comfort and inspiration as you turn its pages.

Thank you for embarking on this journey with me. I hope you enjoy reading it as much as I enjoyed writing it.

Warm regards,

J K Arya

www.ingramcontent.com/pod-product-compliance
Lightning Source LLC
LaVergne TN
LVHW041940070526
838199LV00051BA/2854